Targeting the Mature Traveler

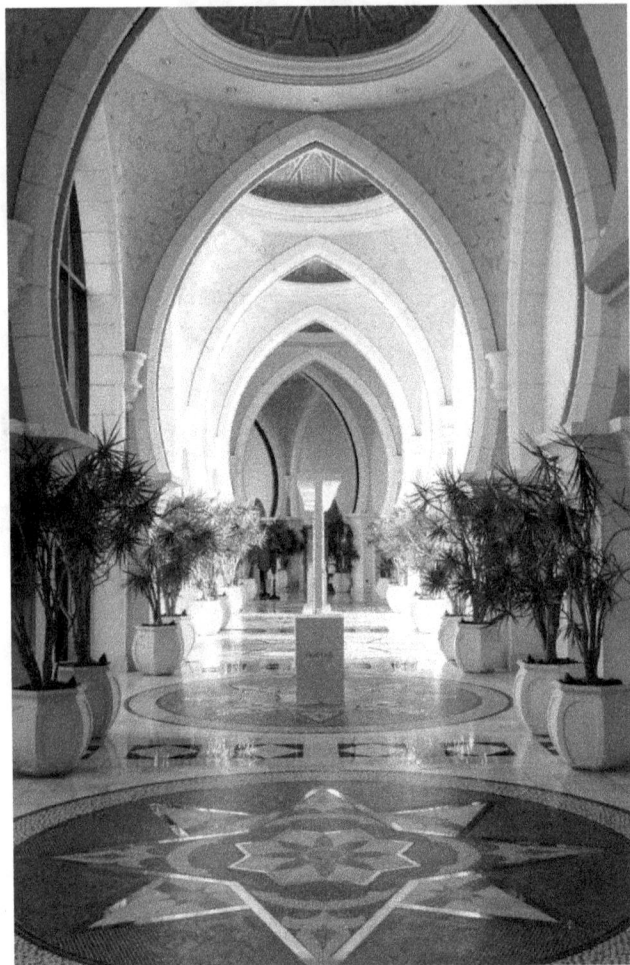

Image 1 Splendid Dubai [Photo by Nick Fewings]

Targeting the Mature Traveler

Developing Strategies for an Emerging Market

Dr Jacqueline Jeynes PhD, MBA, BEd(Hons), BA(Hons)

BEP

BUSINESS EXPERT PRESS

Leader in applied, concise business books

First published in 2021 by
Business Expert Press, LLC
222 East 46th Street, New York, NY 10017
www.businessexpertpress.com

ISBN-13: 978-1-95253-846-9 (paperback)
ISBN-13: 978-1-95253-847-6 (e-book)

Business Expert Press Tourism and Hospitality Management Collection

Collection ISSN: 2375-9623 (print)
Collection ISSN: 2375-9631 (electronic)

Cover design by Charlene Kronstedt
Interior design by S4Carlisle Publishing Services Private Ltd.,
Chennai, India

First edition: 2021

10 9 8 7 6 5 4 3 2 1

Printed in the United States of America.

Description

This book provides a profile of the mature travel market based on recent research by review sites, tour operators and agents, and national press. It identifies recent trends with potential growth in destinations, types of holiday, the criteria holidaymakers use when planning a holiday, and how the final choice is made.

Customer data and global demographic profiles leads to a range of strategic marketing options for those in tourism and travel sectors, and travel trends into 2021 and beyond.

Despite significant changes globally as the coronavirus became a pandemic, the strategic approach identified here still forms a sound basis for taking the industry forward.

Whether you are a student on a travel and tourism course, part of the global travel agency network, a tour operator, or provider of products and services, this book covers the underpinning profile of who the 50+ mature customer is, what they are looking for, and, ultimately, strategies to inform and encourage them to buy in the future.

Keywords

tourism; travel trends; mature traveler; tourist destinations; overtourism; ecotourism; travel agents; tour operators; global demographics; marketing strategy; UGIs; country profiles

Contents

List of Figures

List of Tables

List of Charts

Acknowledgments

As with any book of this nature, there are many people who have provided data, reports on surveys, and help and support throughout the process of bringing such diverse material together.

As a regular writer for Silver Travel Advisor, this was the starting point for my research into the mature travel market, so I am indebted to Debbie Marshall for her support and for giving me access to the latest Silver Travel Report, as well as previous surveys and reports. Others who offered insights into the mature sector include the following:

Salvatore Maniscalco, from Ramblers Cruise & Walk Holidays/ Adagio

Paul Johnson, from the Luxury Travel Blog

Lauren Williams, from the Brighter Group, for suggesting a link with one of their clients, Rocky Mountaineer

Tessa Day, from Rocky Mountaineer, for checking that the information is up to date

Sarah Locke, from Titan Travel, with their excellent Trends 2020 publication

Dawn Walters, for some insights into the Oddfellows Travel Club

Tour operators, such as The Aurora Zone and SmoothRed, who offer packages ideally suited to the mature traveler (based on trends identified)

Gina Dolecki, from USTOA (United States Tour Operators Association), with one of their latest press releases on travel trends from their member survey

There were also several people who provided more detailed information on marketing to the mature traveler, including

Tim Bond, from the Data & Marketing Association (DMA), with some excellent reports on customer engagement and Responsible Marketing

Jeremy, from ATTEST, for access to several reports, including their 2019 Travel Report and the 2019 Trends Across Generations

ADARA Traveler 360 report on Rugby World Cup Fan Travel Insights and discussions about personalization and customer loyalty

Sarah Hein, from Wish Trip, with information on collecting data around visitors' experiences

Jasman Ahmad, from Accord, regarding advertising to mature sectors

Lisa Targett, from TRIBE re Brands

Thanks also go to lots of online sources, of course, particularly the following, where data and/or images have been found.

Statista.com is an excellent resource, with some charts that can be downloaded free, some brief details about international statistics plus some excellent paid-for detailed reports that give still further insights into what is happening worldwide

Unsplash.com—an excellent source of photographs (Unsplash, 2020)

Office for National Statistics UK (ONS)

U.S. Travel Association (ustravel.org)

Travel.trade.com

The Bibliography section lists many sources of further information, but I would like to express my sincere thanks to all those who have contributed in some way, whether you are included in the preceding list or not. Thank you!

Dr Jacqueline Jeynes, 2020

Foreword

At the time of completing this book (January–February 2020), the escalating spread of the coronavirus is having a devastating impact on global travel. This has particularly hit flights and cruise ships with trips canceled and whole regions on a quarantine "lock down." It remains to be seen how this will affect travel and tourism industries around the world. However, having a clearer picture of the demographic profile and preferred travel options of an aging population will help to kick-start the industry as the crisis recedes.

One of the most respected organizations in the UK, Silver Travel Advisor, has 112,000 members who regularly view their website, plus thousands more who follow them on social media channels, including Facebook and Twitter [www.silvertraveladvisor.com]. They note that "Today's 70-year old's show little sign of slowing down."

They have produced an annual Silver Travel Industry Report for five years now, based on survey responses from members—1200 for 2019 Report, 2500 for 2020 Report—including analysis of data from major players in the tourist industry. Although this provides a comprehensive picture of the mature travel market in the UK, it clearly has a broader impact as it highlights trends on a global scale.

Based on UK statistics, the 55+ age sector is the largest group of holidaymakers, making up 35 percent of overseas holidaymakers in 2018. This is the highest of any age group and 17 percent higher than the 25- to 34-year age group. In the United States, 48 percent of customers booking vacations and short trips are 51 to 70 years old, more than double the 20 percent in the 36 to 50 age group [USTOA]. However, note the later discussion about what different client groups are looking for and whether they plan trips independently rather than go via a tour operator. So this is a significant sector to consider when tour operators are deciding their marketing strategy for the future.

A recent survey by *The Mail on Sunday* is very revealing: £9 billion was spent by British travelers with an average trip expenditure of £3216 based on 3.5 trips a year. This is just the UK market, so, clearly, this is a growing potential market, and results are likely to be similar in other countries. In the United States, for example, $17 billion was spent on tourism in 2017 through 2018 [USTOA], baby boomers spending around 27 days a year on travel/vacation. By 2019, U.S. domestic travel increased by 2 percent to $2.29 billion and international travel by $79.6 million, representing a 3.5 percent increase over 2018.

PART 1

Introduction and Mature Traveler Profiles

Why This Book?

The original intention of writing this book was to highlight how much the travel industry has grown, even in just a decade, and its considerable contribution to the global economy. Based in the UK, the starting point for discussion and analysis is from a British perspective. However, this has been extended to include the United States alongside the UK and to further extend the picture across several other major countries where tourism plays a significant role in their economic development.

The GDP (Gross Domestic Product) of every country receives some contribution from tourism, whether this is a small percentage or a major part of the economic viability of the nation. The travel and tourism sectors incorporate much more than holiday resorts, tourist attractions, flights, and travel for both inbound and domestic visitors.

There is a clear link with employment, improving the infrastructure, construction and development of accommodation and business premises. In many countries, the rise in numbers of visitors to historical monuments and ancient structures, for instance, has led to the need for increased efforts to preserve and maintain them, to ensure their fabric is not damaged or destroyed by sheer volume of footfall. We regularly hear of the impact "overtourism" has on a region, often leading to exasperation and resentment by the local population to these invading travelers! Paris and Venice immediately come to mind.

As a travel writer for several years, with a focus on the mature traveler, it has been interesting to see how much the volume of tourists has grown in so many destinations. Queues are longer than ever for attractions even when a timed entry ticket is introduced. For example, the recent

Tutankhamen exhibition in London required up to an hour of extra waiting past the expected entry time, and that was if you were actually at the front of the queue. Once inside, it was so crowded you had to fight your way through the throng to get close enough to see the exhibits.

Feedback, reviews, and blogs were obviously more negative than you would expect for such a special exhibition. Did this make any difference to the organization or the venue? Clearly not, and, to be fair, there was little they could do at this stage apart from warning visitors with prebooked tickets to be prepared for the wait, and to restrict visit time once inside.

On the positive side, from a marketing perspective, the advertising and publicity was extremely successful, leading to demand exceeding capacity. However, a further negative response was because the stunning Tutankhamen Mask was not actually part of the display, although it featured prominently in the promotion literature.

What Has Led to This Rise in Tourism?

The term "bucket list" of destinations you must see before you die (that is, kick the bucket) has come into everyday usage, giving everyone a chance to dream of and plan a series of trips into the future. Of course, how far into the future depends on your age! The list generally includes the same tourist attractions worldwide—see the list of the most visited attractions later in the book—so perhaps this is a good time to carry out research globally to see how the list differs between age groups and geographic location.

A question for marketing professionals may be, "Where does this fit with the notion of a last-minute, spontaneous choice of where to visit next?" How can you attract a customer to a new, different, less popular destination or experience? Evidence from various sources suggests that most people are not so dedicated to just fulfilling the bucket list before anything else, often because these destinations are more expensive or involve a big trip that needs careful planning to make the most from the visit. Thankfully, there are still plenty of opportunities to find and promote exciting new destinations or activities, such as the Aurora Zone trips to find the Northern Lights in the more remote Finnish Lapland rather than Iceland – image 2 shows the Aurora Borealis (Aurora Zone 2019).

Image 2 The aurora borealis [Photo by Sami Takarautio]

A feature of how much tourism has changed is the number of trips or vacations customers are likely to take each year. In the early part of the 20th century in the UK, there would be just one annual family holiday, which meant saving money for a year to be able to afford it. For all but the very wealthy, this holiday would typically be within the UK, often at a seaside resort. It was the 1970s before package holidays overseas, mainly in Spain, became affordable for the wider population.

As we can see in later discussions, we have an aging population globally, with few countries showing a significantly larger younger group, up to the age of 24 and in the 25 to 50 age group, such as India. The term "baby boomer" is used widely, generally referring to 50+ as being the ones with the most disposable income, the wealthiest pensioners ever. This is not actually helpful when you look more closely at the mature travel sector.

Baby boomers, strictly speaking, are those born toward the end of, and in the immediate years following, World War II in 1945. The birthrate naturally spiked as military personnel returned home, the UK seeing the only time 1 million births were recorded in one year, 1947. The rate of births then went down to a more stable level. The next spike of 1 million births was in 1964—babies of baby boomers, so the next generation. Note that the age of mothers was much lower than it is now, as a woman aged over 25 was considered to be an "old" mother biologically.

This later generation had a different social and economic environment as they grew older and now, in their 50s, may indeed have had better private pensions than those who are now over 70 years old. As a mature market sector, it is, therefore, unhelpful to count them as a single target group.

There has been a staggering (not a term I would normally use but appropriate in this case) rise in the range of media channels and the use of social media in particular in just the last five years. Although this was initially associated with younger age groups and the millennials, where it is the norm and a significant part of their everyday life, the rise in the use of iPads and smartphones in the 65+ age group has opened up so many more opportunities for the travel and tourism sectors to reach new customers.

How Do We Tap into this Growing Mature Market?

This book provides a broad picture of the mature travel market starting with demographic profiles. There are many sources referred to here, with a range of different criteria for collecting and collating the data, so some variation in the results is inevitable, although these sources are generally in agreement on the broad picture.

Of particular interest are the sections on choices for booking a trip, where potential customers go to find out more information about a destination in order to make their final choice, and emerging patterns in what they are looking for from a trip. The varied use of social media, reviews, online searches, and hard copy is considered in some detail, identifying some of the most effective ways to reach the mature traveler.

The country profiles consider data on where travelers go to and come from and the types of trip they currently research and/or book. Current trends identify emerging international travel destinations that have the potential to attract new visitors. Finally, this leads to strategies that those in the travel sector need to consider in order to meet the changing, but growing, demands of individuals and families wishing to travel more in the future without causing too much damage to the earth.

Whether you are a student on a university course covering Travel and Tourism, part of the global travel agency network, a tour operator, or provider of other products and services, this book covers the underpinning profile of what is on offer, who the potential customer is within the mature age group of 50+, what they are looking for, and, ultimately, strategies to inform and encourage them to buy. The reference section at the end provides information on those who have contributed to this study and where more detailed examples of successful strategies and methods of targeting the mature travel market can be followed up.

Definitions to Consider

What Do We Mean When We Refer to the "Mature" Traveler?

There are so many ways to describe a mature traveler that it does not present a clear-cut definition from a marketing viewpoint. For instance, many definitions include reference to the 50+ age group, 55+ age group, or maybe 70+. Let us face it, at 50 you are not looking for the same things on holiday as your 75-year-old mother!

Below are some broad profiles to consider:

- may still have children living at home
- grandparents looking for multigeneration trips
- solo travelers across all age groups
- those with some form of disability that makes traveling to a new place more difficult

Depending on individual age or profile, they may:

- be interested in the busy nightclub scene and popular tourist spots
- want to relax at beach and pool resorts
- prefer luxury facilities for spa treatments and relaxation
- be looking for adventure and excitement
- enjoy exploring, trekking longer distances, or just walking locally
- prefer city breaks and are interested in experiencing the local culture
- enjoy river or ocean cruising
- want to visit locations where they can sample food and take part in wine tasting
- look for special interest and hobby breaks, either to take part in activities or visit to learn more

- enjoy art and architecture associated with the place, visiting galleries and studios of local artists
- look for the entertainment available such as the theater, opera, concerts
- want to enjoy slower forms of travel such as the train or coach
- be looking for something different, new experiences and destinations
- prefer to book a complete package rather than an ad hoc list of separate elements
- the bucket list! Still have a list of things they must do at some time

We cannot assume that the older age groups are immobile. Also note that solo travel features across many age groups.

A more detailed breakdown is provided by Silver Travel Advisor in their 2020 Report (Silver Travel Advisor 2020). They have identified significant differences within the mature sector, not necessarily related to a specific age group but more closely related to their individual circumstances. These categories are particularly useful when considering strategies to target the sector and to align the product or service more closely with their individual needs.

The categories were developed over time and based on experiences of those who subscribe to Silver Travel Advisor. Note that this is not a travel agency but an online site that offers ideas and insights into travel and activities enjoyed by the more mature traveler. Its success is built on the reviews posted by members (moderated but not paid for) and links with many tour operators and service providers catering specifically for this target group.

Sandwich generation—those with both teenage children and elderly parents to consider. They are likely to take vacations during school or university holiday breaks.

Empty nesters—often work into their 60s, with no children now living at home. They are likely to have a bucket list, look for luxuries, and take multiple holidays over the year, including short breaks. They are also interested in expedition cruises, safari trips, and other new experiences.

Golden oldies—retired, often grandparents, spending up to £20,000 on travel each year. The survey shows they like to take lots of holidays, including short breaks, worldwide travel, city breaks, cruising, and escorted trips—similar findings to those of the Titan Travel survey (Titan Travel 2019–2020).

Multigeneration family—a mix of generations who holiday together and may be retired, working, or in education. They are often looking for big holidays to celebrate birthdays and other significant events. They want unique experiences to make "memories" such as private tours, personal service, short breaks, often staying in the UK; 29 percent of respondents have taken a multigeneration break in the last five years (Silver Travel Advisor 2020).

Single by circumstance—this category includes those who travel on their own, not by choice but often widowed, divorced, or separated from a previous partner. Likely to have high disposable income—although note that if widowed or divorced, they may not have as high a disposable income as they might have had as a couple.

Single by choice—The survey found that around 68 percent of solo travelers are single (for various reasons) and 32 percent have a partner but choose to travel alone (Silver Travel Advisor 2020). Feedback shows that this group of solo travelers may be working or have taken early retirement and are likely to have a higher income available for travel. They are often willing to travel as part of singles groups with interest in self-development; therapy; holistic, learning, and themed breaks; active and adventure breaks.

Note that there were 8.2 million people living alone in the UK in 2018 to 2019, forming a significant market sector (ONS, 2018–2019).

Happy home birds—an interesting definition that may well be reflected in other countries globally. They are mainly retired from employment; like to holiday in their home country; and enjoy coach tours, Christmas events, family holidays, and returning to favorite places.

Less mobile—note that a disability may not always be visible or mobility related. 50 percent of people registered disabled in UK are over 65 years old, and 72 percent of wheelchair users are over 60. Depending on the criteria used, 44 percent of UK pensioners have some form of disability. The "Purple Pound" relates to the spending power of the disabled market and their families, currently thought to be £249 billion. Of course, within this group there is a considerable range of finance levels available to spend on nonessentials.

As we can see, these broad definitions and assumptions may not fit the profile of all mature travelers globally, but they do give a clear picture of the current UK mature travel market. Although we do not want to restrict the opportunity to extend a customer base, we have to start somewhere before we can overcome any stereotypical image of what "mature" represents.

Demographic Profiles

Demographic profiles are produced by every country on the basis of official births, deaths, and, sometimes, a regular census—every 10 years in the UK for example. They are usually broken down into categories such as those in Table 1, sometimes with more detailed profiles about gender, marital status, and those who have reached 100 years of age.

Table 1 World demographic summary by age group 2020 [worldometers .info/demographic]

Age	World (%)	USA (%)	Canada (%)	Australia (%)	Japan (%)	China (%)	India (%)	Germany (%)	UK (%)
0–24	40.97	31.51	27.31	31.50	21.70	39.48	44.17	24.31	29.3
25–54	40.59	39.10	40.49	40.64	37.74	46.30	41.42	38.93	40.3
55–64	9.11	12.75	14.10	11.64	12.16	12.25	7.84	15.07	12.2
65+	9.33	16.63	18.10	16.21	28.40	11.97	6.57	21.69	18.2
55+	18.44	29.38	32.20	27.85	40.56	24.22	14.41	36.76	30.4

For us, the main categories are those over 50, in some profiles over 55, as these are deemed to make up the mature travel sector. As a general picture, the chart shows between a quarter and a third of most nations have a significant population over 55 years old, more than the world average of 18.44 percent. The exception in this demographic profile for 2020 is India, which is well below the average at just over 14 percent.

The World demographic table (Table 1) gives a clear picture of national profiles according to age of the population. This is a sample of nations to indicate differences and similarities between population profiles compared with the global average, so other national profiles are available on the Worldometers website (Worldometers 2020). They also provide several demographic summaries based on criteria other than age.

In this example of country profiles, India has a higher proportion of GenerationZ and millennials than the world average. Older age groups of over 55 have declined to 14.41 percent, fewer than the world average at over 18 percent. All the other nations included in this sample exceed the proportion at 65+ by a significant amount, particularly Japan, at 28.4 percent, and Germany, at almost 22 percent. Germany is seen to have an interesting demographic profile, with a much lower birthrate than others and twice the world average in the 55+ age group.

The Silver Travel Industry Report 2020 is their fifth annual report based on a growing number of respondents from their membership base. It incorporates statistics from various sources as well as specific responses from survey participants. It therefore presents a detailed, comprehensive picture of the UK population demographic. The general picture shows that

75 percent of respondents are in their 50s and 60s.
62 percent are married, with a partner.
61 percent are retired from work/employment.

In 2020, 30 percent of the UK population is over 55 years old, and by 2030, 50 percent of all UK adults will be over 50. This is a significant rise in the proportion of people over 50, which has implications for all sectors of the community, both socially and financially. If you look more closely at the rate of growth in these older age groups, you notice a constant rise evident over each decade, and projections by the Office of National Statistics (ONS), as well as other government sources, reaffirm this trend.

In 2007, 15.9 percent of the population were over 65, rising to 18 percent by 2017, and in 2027 this is likely to rise to 20 percent (see Table 2).

Table 2 Projected rise in number of UK population 65+ years old

2007–2027	% population 65+
2007	15.9
2017	18
2027	20

Staying with the UK demographic profile, the actual number of individuals in each age group shows an interesting spread. Table 3 shows that there are almost 24 million people over 50, with 8.85 million 50 to 60 years old and a further 7.07 million 60 to 70 years old—a substantial sector of the population that still actively takes holidays/vacations and enjoys a wide range of activities (Silver Travel Advisor 2020).

Table 3 Number of UK population in millions

Age group	Number in UK 2020 (in millions)
50–59 years old	8.85
60–69 years old	7.07
70–79 years old	5.29
80–90 years old	2.65

This profile is further supported by the Mature Marketing Association (MMA) as part of their ongoing research into mature market sectors for a range of product and service providers, not just those in the travel sector. They note that there are 23 million over-50s in the UK (MMA) representing 33 percent of the population, 31 percent of the UK workforce, and who are estimated to own 80 percent of the disposable income available.

Other sources of data related to the demographic profile include Gransnet, one of the biggest online communities in the UK, with 300,000 members who are grandparents. It was developed as a follow-on to their successful Mumsnet, a site for mums of any age with children still living at home. Gransnet provides information, guidance, and support for anyone who is a grandparent through regular news features, forum discussions, and surveys. They work with many partner organizations that target this demographic to provide data based on regular surveys of members.

There are 14 million grandparents in the UK, and their average age is 49 (Crisp 2019) (www.gransnet.com). Their demographic breakdown shows the majority, 67 percent, of Gransnet members are aged 55 to 64, with the 65 to 80 age group making up a further 30 percent—see Table 4. They also note that around 75 percent of their members use the social media platform Facebook regularly.

Table 4 *Age profile of Gransnet subscribers*

Age of Gransnet subscribers	
55–64 Mature	67%
65–80 Baby boomers	30%
Over 80	3%

Estimates show there will be 20.4 million aged over 65 by 2041, representing over a quarter of the UK population in just 20 years from now (Keeley 2019) (Travel weekly). A further point related to the growing mature population is that the majority of CEOs in UK are aged over 50 and that in many professions, particularly those in service sectors, there is growing alarm that such a high proportion of the working population will be nearing retirement around the same time. This picture is similar to that in the United States, where there are currently around 40 million over-50s.

This has practical implications for companies that need to replace experienced, knowledgeable staff at higher levels in the organization as well as the need to train new staff or, indeed, to recruit from what may be a dwindling pool of young professionals coming forward. For governments facing a similar situation globally, this has significant financial and social implications. However, the profiles of what the mature sectors are looking for when planning to travel suggests that this opens up a wider potential market because the number of people with more time and money available will inevitably grow.

What Are They Looking For?

As we have seen, this is a diverse group of customers, so it is vital that they are not just "lumped together" under the heading of the mature travel sector (Keeley 2019). Although evidence suggests that 30 percent of over-50s spend more than £3000 per trip on holidays, it also shows that around 12 percent spent at least £5000 on holidays in 2018 (Mail Metro Media Travel Team 2019).

The number of trips they take is also significant, particularly in relation to the spend per trip. The Silver Travel Report 2020 gives a more detailed picture of the number of trips taken by UK respondents. Responses suggest that more than three-quarters take at least one break away from home each year, plus maybe one or two others, with figures staying consistent over this period. Note that respondents may have chosen more than 4 trips and more than 5 trips combined, depending on how they interpreted the question, so more than 100 percent total is recorded (Table 5).

Table 5 Number of trips taken per year 2019–2020

Number of trips three or more nights each year	2019 survey (%)	2020 survey (%)
1–3 trips	77	78
4 or more	23	19
5 or more	11	11

These figures show that by 2020 they were spending a little less than the previous year in the £1000 to £3000 per person bracket. More people are searching for trips at less than £1000 per person, but high-end spending of £5000 or more per person remains stable at 12 percent. Luxury breaks are clearly holding their own, and a recent poll by Classic FM Radio found 88 percent of listeners listed luxury holidays as their top preference.

Although this is the average spend, which differs according to which demographic profile and source of data is used, it represents a formidable opportunity in the UK alone.

However, the things potential customers look for when choosing a holiday, based on their individual ranking of elements (note this is not 100 percent total as they could rank several options), are consistent across various sources of data. Silver Travel Advisor respondents noted that "cheapest price" was least important and decisions of what to book were identified in the same order as those in the Travel Weekly survey 2019:

71 percent said previous good experience with a tour company or holiday destination was a factor in choosing their next holiday/ vacation.

54 percent noted Air Travel Organiser's Licence (ATOL) protection was the first or second most important factor when choosing (a critical issue in early 2020 as the travel industry tries to deal with the impact of COVID-19).

48 percent said the reputation of the provider was an important factor.

46 percent identified good customer service as important.

It is also useful to look at the main motivators when choosing which travel company to book with (Table 6). While around 17 percent paid little or no attention to the brand, and can therefore, potentially, be swayed in their choice, whereas 79 percent consider the brand very seriously (26 percent) or to some extent (53 percent)—also see later section on shopping habits.

Table 6 Reasons for choosing to book with a particular brand

Reasons behind choice	2019 (%)	2020 (%)
Previous good experience with the brand	71	45
ATOL protection		32
Company reputation	48	
Customer service	46	20
Choice of destination available	45	38
Recommendations	33	25

In the 2020 Report, there is a broader spread of criteria that motivates them to make their choice compared with the 2019 survey and several options to choose in some of the survey questions. Despite all these factors, previous good experience with the company remains the top criterion overall.

Major differences appear in the importance of ATOL protection, presumably linked to recent difficulties and collapse of some major players in the tourism industry. Customer service has ranked at just 20 percent in this latest survey, which may, or may not, reflect improvements in support provided to customers.

The Travel Weekly survey also allowed several options to be chosen when considering their preferred type of holiday (Travel Weekly 2019). Results from this survey show that:

45 percent said city breaks were their favorite option

42 percent were looking for country house hotels within the UK—up from 37 percent in the previous survey

33 percent still opt for beach holidays

The Mail large-scale surveys found that for the 58+ age group, sea cruises were still a favorite ranking higher than beach resorts, lakes, and mountains. The United States has also seen a growing river cruise market since 2018 (Mail Metro Media Travel Team 2019). It is useful to note that 48 percent of *Mail* readers class themselves as well traveled, so they know what they are looking for and have lots of experience to draw on when deciding where to go. Yet they are still open to new suggestions and are willing to try something different as their next travel experience.

The Silver Travel Report 2020 gives a more detailed breakdown of what type of break respondents are looking for. The biggest rise in trips they are considering has been in adventure holidays (up from 7 to 25 percent), cultural trips (up from 21 to 34 percent), and luxury markets (up from 11 to 21 percent). Table 7 shows the difference in choices between 2019 and 2020.

Table 7 Type of break they are looking for in 2019–2020

Type of vacation	2019 preference list (%)	2020 preference list (%)
City breaks	45	47
Beach holidays	33	43
UK breaks	30	30
All-inclusive	27	36
Cultural tours	21	34
Luxury	11	21
Adventure	7	25

Factors Related to Type of Break

Factors related to the type of holiday being considered, though clearly this varies considerably according to the individual traveler, generally fall within the following main categories.

City Breaks

City breaks appear consistently near the top of the "to do" list in many surveys. For instance, the most-booked places to visit in 2019, identified by Trip Advisor, support this reference to the continuing popularity of city breaks, particularly, though not exclusively, in Europe (Trip Advisor 2019). Trip Advisor is a major source of information and advice for travelers worldwide. They identified the 10 most popular destinations booked through them, or reviewed on their website, in 2019 as primarily Europe, with three out of 10 being trips to the United States.

The attraction often quoted by the mature traveler is the opportunity to explore outside of the busy tourist attractions, to stroll around the quieter streets, and see more of the local culture.

Ocean Cruising

Ocean cruising continues to grow in popularity with the mature traveler, whether as a solo, couple, or intergeneration group. Previously considered to be at the luxury end of the market, and obviously some cruise lines still pride themselves on this element, there is now a growing range of options promoted in the lower price range, adding to demand.

Two million people from the UK booked an ocean cruise in 2018, citing the main attraction as the range of destinations on offer (61 percent rated this the highest issue in 2019, up to 76 percent in 2020), and around two-thirds said they would consider going to a new destination. Overall, 92 percent said they would choose another ocean cruise (Silver Travel Advisor 2020). However, Condor Ferries (Condor Ferries 2020), offering shorter ferry trips and cruises from and around the UK, found that the first factor customers cited when choosing their trip was the price, followed by reviews, with 65 percent booking over the phone on the same day. The general picture was that customers book between one and three months before the planned trip.

In the 50+ group, only around one-third have been on an ocean cruise, with the majority of clients in the 60+ age group, representing a potential market to tap into. The U.S. travel market noted (2019) that 30 percent of baby boomers opt for a cruise.

Many are now looking for smaller cruise ships, whether they have cruised before or not, as the massive cruise liners feel "impersonal, too crowded, and you cannot get to some destinations because they are too big." Cruising is seen as a positive option for the solo traveler—41 percent aged over 65 said they were likely to go on a cruise at some time (Solo Traveler World 2019) provided single supplements were not too great.

Note that as cruise liners get bigger, with much more to offer as on-board entertainment and facilities, this may alter the balance of customer profiles, which may or may not be seen as a positive step for some.

River Cruising

The latest research from Titan Travel (Titan Travel 2019–2020) found that the cruising market is changing as more smaller cruise ships come into service. These are ideal for river cruising, of course, but also smaller ships on longer routes can get closer to ports than many of the ocean liners. This opens up new opportunities, with more trips considered to have a focus on exploring or being more adventurous than before, such as in Alaska, and allows some relief from overtourism in hotspots we have seen.

The destinations on offer are the critical factor in customer choice, with the opportunity to see so many different places in a shorter time—and only unpack once—still the main attraction for 70 percent of respondents. 23 percent of them had been on a river cruise before, with a significant majority, 74 percent in 2019, rising to 93 percent in 2020, who would choose to do another. The main reason stated by 40 percent of respondents who had not taken a river cruise was the perception that it was too expensive (Silver Travel Advisor 2020).

Spa and Well-being

The growth in spa, relaxation, and well-being facilities has generally been in the luxury sector. In the UK, for instance, these facilities are incorporated into most high-end hotels and resorts (see Image 3).

Image 3 A spa venue [Photo by Taylor Simpson]

With a focus on healing and well-being at spa resorts, both the 50+ and 65+ client groups may have different expectations of, and attitudes toward, more cosmetic treatments being introduced at many established facilities globally. This is echoed in the later section on popular and new destinations.

Rail Travel

Rail travel is a growing area, considered more environmentally friendly than other forms of transport. Various surveys find that customers regularly state they prefer other forms of transport to air travel, mainly because they do not enjoy the airport experience. This is clearly something that needs to be addressed as it is a common statement whenever travelers are asked for preferences.

Rail travel is ideal for those preferring a more sustainable travel option where the journey, not the destination, is the focus. It is the direct opposite of air travel, where the flight is generally viewed as a necessity. Identified as one of the big trends for the future, long-distance sleeper trains are particularly appealing to the mature traveler, not least because of the slower pace, high-end luxury facilities needed to ensure a comfortable journey, and therefore the higher price.

Coach Trips

The biggest influencers of the decision to book a coach trip are word-of-mouth and online reviews such as those on Silver Travel Advisor or Trip Advisor websites, plus value for money. The choice of destination is important, of course, as is prime location of hotels, home pickups, a good tour guide, and onboard Wi-Fi. The main things stated as negative views about coach tours were related to spending too long on the coach each day, a packed itinerary that does not include the occasional relaxed day with no traveling, and a definite preference for *no* background music!

The Staycation

The "staycation"—staying in your home country rather than traveling overseas—is a growing UK market, as it is in other countries. For example, figures from the United States show that 66 percent of Americans were planning a domestic spring vacation in 2018–2019. The Association of British Travel Agents (ABTA) Holiday Habits 2019 (ABTA 2019) report notes that 56 percent were planning a domestic break, with UK customers taking two staycations per annum, 35 percent of these opting for seaside breaks.

Factors Related to Customer Profiles

Factors related to customer preferences, as defined in the earlier discussion of demographic profiles, add an extra dimension to choices made by those planning a trip. The Oddfellows Travel Club 2019 small-scale survey found 53 percent of members will generally travel as a couple, 42 percent as a solo traveler, the remaining 5 percent in other combinations such as part of a group (Oddfellows 2019). The main factors that are relevant to the final choice include multigeneration groups, solo travelers, and the need for accessible travel.

Multigeneration Holidays

There are 14 million grandparents in the UK. In the Silver Travel Report, 29 percent of respondents said they had previously taken a multigeneration break, and three-quarters of those said they would do so again. In their recent survey of subscribers to website Gransnet (Crisp 2019), 64 percent of them said they would consider a multigeneration holiday, 25 percent of these also paying for the child/children accompanying them.

Beach holidays were still the most popular choice for these respondents, followed by villas that gave more space and freedom to each of the varied age groups present. They all said that the range of activities available, and separate spaces for quiet time, were the crucial factors in order to keep everyone happy.

Solo Travelers

Solo travel is growing in popularity across all age groups, but certainly among the mature sectors that are looking for more adventurous trips, often as escorted trips rather than organizing each element independently. The attraction is not just related to organizing the details but gives the solo traveler a chance to meet others traveling alone and not feel out of place.

This market is growing at around 10 percent year on year and makes up approximately 15 percent of the holiday market.

Booking.com analysis shows that 40 percent of those in the 55 to 64 age group who book through them took a trip alone in 2019. People searching via Google for "solo travel" has seen a 130 percent increase in the last year, and #solotravel on Instagram had 5 million posts in 2019. Security and safety appeared to be the biggest issue for solo travelers in 2019, but in 2020 this was overtaken by the chance to meet new people with shared interests.

Accessible Travel

In July 2018, the Package Travel Regulations in the UK required travel and cruise companies selling more than one component of a holiday to provide full information on accessibility of these products for different types of impairments.

Not all disabilities/impairments are visible, of course. Around 11 million people in the UK are deaf or hard of hearing and so have to watch information boards for flights at airports because they cannot hear announcements clearly. Given the aging population numbers, dementia is a growing concern with 850,000 sufferers in the UK, likely to rise to 2.1 million by 2025. The majority of travelers needing more accessible travel will also be accompanied by a carer or other family members.

How Potential Customers Carry Out Preliminary Research

Around a third of customers (34 percent) research travel review sites, and more than half of them (55 percent) refer to such sites before making the final choice of destination or package; 48 percent of respondents say they refer to friends and family when thinking about possible holiday choices, and 21 percent see them as part of their research activity.

Although many read reviews posted by others before they decide, there is also evidence that suggests older groups are less likely to be influenced by reviews and prefer to make their own decisions. Research by Oddfellows Travel Club showed that 52 percent of customers searched online, a significant 43 percent chose to go back to where they had stayed before, and 41 percent asked family and friends about their own experiences.

Chart 1 shows how customers use a laptop or phone to research destinations and make bookings, based on which device they think is the most useful for each activity. As you might expect, the laptop (or PC) is the preferred option when carrying out research on brands or destinations, with nearly three-quarters of potential customers using it to plan and book travel or accommodation. Once traveling, the phone is an easier option to check in, pick up a rental vehicle, or book the extra activities while away from home.

Just over half (51 percent) of research activity relates to accommodation or airline websites directly, 23 percent using comparison sites, with 60 percent saying they also look through these sites for inspiration. Although fewer than 18 percent carry out research by following up advertisements and travel articles, these are a critical element when looking for inspiration, especially at earlier stages of decision-making.

Example: Luxury Travel Blog (Johnson 2020) posts regular features on travel, destinations, top-end accommodation, and facilities and has a

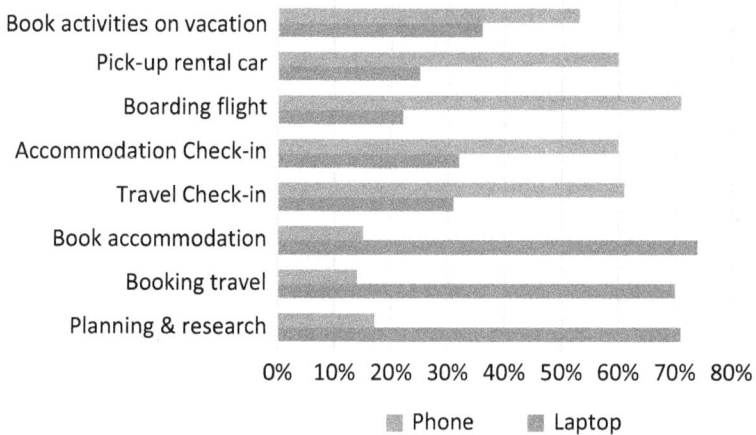

Chart 1 *How travelers use technology when planning a trip (statista .com)*

following from both potential customers and those in the travel industry. A recent summary of the profile of those who visit the site shows a clear delineation between younger and older groups for this particular platform (www.aluxurytravelblog.com), though not necessarily for what is on offer there. Although the majority of visitors to the site are in the younger age groups up to 54 years old, there is still a significant 20 percent of visitors in the mature sector who want to find out more about luxury travel.

42 percent aged 18 to 34
38 percent aged 35 to 54
20 percent aged 55 to 65+

Online Reviews

Evidence from Data Marketing Association (DMA 2019) found that 40 to 44 percent of people state they trust customer reviews and testimonials and that "expert" opinion is still important during this research phase. The big "but" about these statements is the earlier research from Gransnet that suggests that less than 1 percent of their subscribers take any notice of celebrity endorsements (Crisp 2019) because they are being paid to promote a product or service. Not a good marketing investment, then!

Reviews are clearly a significant factor for all age groups, with evidence from the MMA suggesting that reference to online reviews is the norm for younger groups (up to 55 years old) regardless of the product or service (DMA 2019; MMA).

Example: on a recent trip to Nice with a group of friends around 50 years old, they all automatically "googled" places and products to see what others had said before making any decisions about buying. The question is really whether this is the same for those in the 60 to 70 age group.

The last few years have seen a significant rise in online review sites aimed at the travel industry. Trip Advisor has been particularly successful in expanding its reach, their logo easily recognized at hotels and restaurants globally and on company websites. However, their recent change toward becoming a booking agent rather than just a review site has changed perceptions of its impartiality and the weightings used to publish reviews. Given the volume of reviews posted internationally, some form of weighting must be in place. Recent publicity suggests there could be a significant number of reviews posted online that are not objective, written by either staff or family members. It is difficult to judge, but longer, more detailed reviews based on a clearly defined visit date are a preferred option.

Other review sites are also growing in popularity—Booking.com, Trivago, and Expedia, for instance. Despite this, the most popular site for mature travel reviews in the UK is Silver Travel Advisor, with over 112,000 regular readers. It received the Silver (2nd place) award as the Best Online Review Site in 2018 and Gold award (1st place) in 2019, overtaking Trip Advisor in the national public vote.

An important point to remember is that Silver Travel Advisor is specifically aimed at the mature traveler, so its popularity also reflects the growing cohort of people willing to make buying decisions based on someone else's views.

Questions about the Impact of Reviews

How useful do potential customers find them?

Who posts them? (a recent comment from an Airbnb provider was that "the older ones always want to write an essay in their review rather than just a quick response!")

Are they moderated in some way? This is not always clear from the site where they are posted.

And are they really genuine reviews? This has become an issue recently because reports have suggested there is some question about validity.

While many of the factors included in reviews are subjective and based on a particular moment or place, they generally present an overall evaluation. Most importantly, they often identify very poor service or facilities plus the inevitable disaster scenario—probably the biggest factor in choices made rather than whether they get a "good" or "very good" rating.

Shorter reviews, such as those on booking.com, ask a specific set of questions with limited space for personal comments, so there is some consistency in the scope of responses. Tour operators and service providers regularly ask customers for reviews, often just a quick 1-star to 5-star rating and limited comments. And, of course, we have incitement to comment printed on receipts on anything from restaurants and entertainment to holiday supplies.

The later section that considers buying habits in more detail adds to the picture, but it is also useful to discuss the extent to which reviews actually influence the final decision to buy.

Is the Purchasing Decision Influenced by What Others Say about a Place?

Reviews are seen as a powerful marketing tool by organizations, a low-cost way to increase potential sales through recommendation by previous customers. User-generated images (UGIs) are rapidly being seen as a significant marketing tool to increase viewer time on the website and exploration of what is on offer (Gurney 2020).

Alternatively, reviews may be included as an information service on behalf of providers, giving potential customers ideas about options they would otherwise not consider. Feedback in reviews may also highlight areas of service or facilities that need improvement by the organization. However, it is not clear whether, or the extent to which, such negative comments are taken on board by the provider or influence future strategic decisions.

Who Posts Them?

Every visit to a restaurant, hotel, or theater results in a request for feedback that may be used for marketing purposes, so reviews can be written by individual customers. As a regular contributor to Silver Travel Advisor, the author's emphasis throughout is how a particular experience could be enjoyed by the mature traveler, generally written from a couple's perspective, or out with friends, rather than as a solo traveler. Although there is reference to potential issues for those with reduced mobility, this is not the primary focus.

Example: A visit to three hotels owned by the same group (such as those in Gozo Malta or in the Algarve Portugal) shows how different each is, the location, and what attractions there are nearby (Silver Travel Advisor 2020).

In some cases, description of what a trip involves is often based on copy that reflects what a venue/location says it has to offer rather than reporting back on a visit to confirm what the visitor will find. For instance, problems are regularly identified in reviews when building work is still going on at a venue, but the planned image of what it will look like when completed is on the website.

When researching a potential destination, the choice will be influenced by the more serious complaints identified by the mature traveler in their feedback after a trip. Table 8 suggests that perhaps previous feedback on the standard of accommodation, meals, and customer service have been taken on board by providers, given the significant decrease in the number of travelers listing these as the most important complaints about their vacation. However, the issue of hidden costs and the "single

Table 8 Common complaints found in reviews

Complaint	2019 (%)	2020 (%)
Standard of accommodation	42	16
Poor customer service	32	
Standard of meals	27	7
Poor/nonexistent Wi-Fi	21	12
Hidden costs		21
Single supplement		17

supplement" are becoming a real issue for the mature market (Silver Travel Advisor 2020). This is considered further in later discussion about concerns that need to be considered by providers.

Where to Find Inspiration to Decide Where to Go?

Friends and family are crucial at all stages of the planning process, and often the main source of inspiration at the very early stage of drawing up a list of potential places to visit. When asked in a survey, respondents state that Internet searches remain the top source of inspiration for travelers when they are at the early stages of deciding where to go. Printed brochures remain popular because they have a longer shelf life, and reviews by others (30 percent use reviews for "inspiration") are a critical element of first-stage decision-making.

The Titan Travel survey shows very clearly how the mature sector uses IT when researching and booking vacations, echoed by Statista analysis in Table 9. At the early stages of making a booking decision, a popular source of inspiration remains the printed brochure, despite many tour operators considering ending their use (the Titan Travel report quotes TUI Group who originally planned to get rid of them by 2020 but have since reversed this decision).

Table 9 Sources of information to help customers decide what to book

Medium used	2019 (%)	2020 (%)
Internet search	37	63
Online review sites	15	45
Hard-copy brochures (posted)	10	16
Where been before/through travel agent they already know	10	10
Family and friends' recommendation	9	37

Titan Travel has seen a 43 percent increase in requests for brochures, so, clearly, this is still a positive and effective marketing tool. As noted previously, the brochure has a longer shelf life than advertisements in other media to tempt the consumer. Potential travelers use the physical nature of the information, illustrations, and copy about places to visit, in a more exploratory way to get new ideas. They keep returning to the printed word to check details, and, because a trip often includes someone else, it is also easier to share a brochure. It is clear from various data sources that personal recommendation from family and friends about possible destinations is key and that more than half of over 55-year-olds cite this as the main source of inspiration.

The Silver Travel Report also asked respondents what sort of images they preferred to see as an incentive to travel to a new destination. The majority were not interested in seeing photographs of people in a resort, or wintry scenes. Only 10 percent liked to see images of cruise ships, and then only if they were already interested in cruising; 36 percent preferred to see photographs of the resort itself; and 31 percent just scenic views (without people). The UGIs discussed earlier are growing in importance for both providers who incorporate them into their websites and marketing materials and individual Blog posts by potential "influencers" (Gurney 2020).

Factors that appear to influence the choice of destination include a range of options that give added value to the trip.

Food and wine tastings are growing in popularity, both in the growing UK wine and spirits production areas and in overseas wine regions.

Visits to new, unusual attractions as well as the better-known ones.

Activities made easy, such as longer distance walking with someone to transport your luggage between overnight accommodation each day.

Those who want to arrange their own walking route, such as the Wye Valley Way in Wales, rely on websites for accommodation to be easy to use and to book well in advance to match their itinerary (Jeynes 2017).

Emphasis on environmentally friendly offerings are particularly important as we go into the 2020s. Whatever format this takes, it is potentially a deciding factor (Condé Nast 2019; US Travel Association 2019).

Options for Booking a Journey or Event

There are a growing number of options available for customers to book a journey or event, some of which are more appealing to the mature traveler, although this depends on many factors and not just age group.

Face to face with a travel agent—31 percent of UK travelers (Travel Weekly) still prefer to complete the final booking with a travel agent. Among the reasons quoted are that it is quicker and easier to make sure the whole package is booked at the same time, which may suggest there are still some aspects of online booking that people struggle with. Security of payment is mentioned regularly as an issue of online booking (Keeley 2019).

Those who use hard-copy brochures often keep them for the full length of the brochure's life rather than single use. They are expensive to produce and post, but they are seen as recognition of client loyalty and a reminder of options they may have been considering previously.

Mailing lists for regular distribution of brochures include existing customers, but brochures can be requested by visitors to the tour operator's website and so are likely to be used for inspiration as well as information. Customers often use brochures from different operators to compare what is available before completing their booking online.

Search and book online—potential new customers carry out research on what is available online, before going on to make a booking. This can include:

Hotels and accommodation—the most popular sites in the UK include Booking.com, Trivago, Laterooms.com, and Expedia.com worldwide.

Hotel chains' websites, especially those for loyal customers offering special membership deals.

Transport—Trainline.com includes travel across the UK and EU countries and is broadening the scope of what people can book through them.

Local bus and train companies are developing apps and their websites to make it easier for customers to "google" or use other search engines to find what they want.

Tour operators are still a popular source of bookings via their websites.

Online is still the leading booking route, with 58 percent of respondents (Silver Travel Advisor 2020) booking straightforward breaks themselves. For more complex trips, such as cruises or escorted tours, 36 percent in 2020 (31 percent 2019) use a travel agent, similar to previous years. Within these statistics, 64 percent book online direct with the travel company.

Although Chart 2 is based on 2016 figures, it gives a picture of the breakdown of bookings for hotels, package holidays, and vacation rentals, with hotels taking the number one spot for volume and value of online bookings.

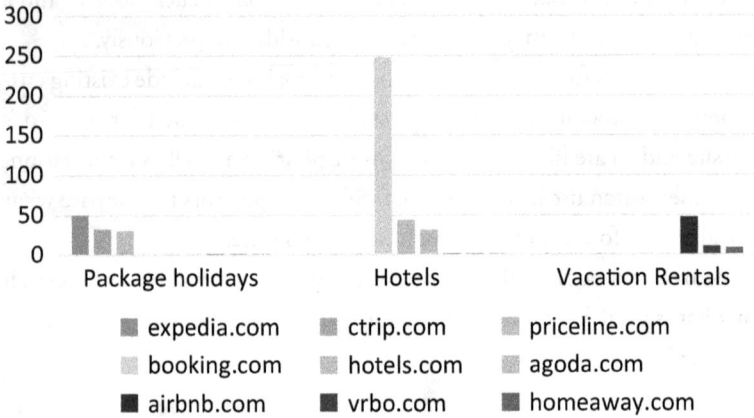

Chart 2 Online travel market for booking a trip

Legend:
- expedia.com
- booking.com
- airbnb.com
- ctrip.com
- hotels.com
- vrbo.com
- priceline.com
- agoda.com
- homeaway.com

Online Shopping Habits

Given the potential options available to customers identified earlier, and before we consider individual country profiles with data related to inbound or outbound travel trends, it is useful to consider online shopping habits in a bit more detail. This will help to place the role and scope of online shopping generally into the context of marketing for the tourism and travel industries, discussed later in Part 3: Strategies for reaching the mature traveler.

The general picture for online shopping, according to recent research from TRIBE—who offer "a team of marketing experts [to] connect some of the biggest brands on the planet with consumers the world over"—is that 87 percent of the population research products or services online (Targett 2019). Around 86 percent, a substantial majority, state they mainly research online when looking for entertainment events and

restaurants, thus particularly for leisure activities. When looking specifically at the mature market, 83 percent of baby boomers (their definition
as those over 50 years old) buy products or services online, and 68 percent
over 55 years old buy something online every month, indicating that both
groups now consider online shopping a viable option when researching a
product or service.

The Mail Metro Media group, the biggest UK news brand, reaches
over 35 million readers a month. Their 2019 research results make interesting reading in the context of travel planning (Mail Metro Media Travel
Team 2019). Research across 11 million of their daily readers shows that
press adverts and articles about travel have a vital input into the final
choice. They found that 44 percent said such information effectively
changes their perception of a brand and what it can offer, and more than
half say that advertisements and articles add to their understanding of
what a travel company offers. They do, therefore, have a potential impact
on buying decisions.

Given that 18.2 million of their readers are planning a break in the
next 12 months (2020), these factors must clearly form part of every tour
operator's strategic plans for the future. Although a breakdown of in-
fluences may be different for younger travelers (note later points about
building brand loyalty), this reflects what is significant for the growing
mature travel groups in their late 50s.

The 2019 survey on Buying Habits from ATTEST, an online consumer research organization (ATTEST 2019) adds a further dimension.
It shows a direct inverse relationship between using an app or browser
and age group. So, whereas 75.4 percent of millennials aged 25 to 39
(their definition) prefer to use an app to research and buy products or services, 52.8 percent of mature shoppers would much rather use an Internet
browser on a phone or PC. Another clear distinction is drawn between
age groups when asked whether they have bought something online when
they were drunk. Only around 15 percent in the oldest age group, 65 to
80+, owned up to doing so, but 31 percent of young buyers aged 18 to
24 and a significant 42 percent of millennials said they had done this
(no indication of whether the purchases had been appropriate or not in
the survey).

Although the Buying Habits survey covers all age groups, there are some useful findings. As we noted earlier on the role of reviews, it appears that receiving a bad review from existing or previous customers does impact on whether they are keen to continue buying a brand. For instance, over a third of "mature" customers and those in the 65+ age group said they stopped buying a brand after bad reviews were published. It would seem that a much greater proportion of the 18- to 39-year-old group are more sensitive to online reviews, because 38 percent of these younger groups and 34 percent of millennials stop buying following a bad review.

Brand loyalty is a further issue to consider in relation to buying habits (also see later section on strategies), as the ATTEST survey shows: brand loyalty is still very important to customers, and many choose not to switch unless there is a very pressing reason to do so (Table 10).

Table 10 Brand loyalty based on age group

Brand loyalty—age group	% loyal to brand
18–24	63
25–49 including millennials	57
50–64 Mature	47
65–80+	46

The importance of customer support was also a significant factor in whether customers stay loyal to a brand, with similar ratings for all age groups, at around 55 to 65 percent, saying it was important to them.

E-mails continue to be the best way for potential customers to receive information and marketing from brands, with 60 percent saying this was a preferred means. This may differ from several other research sources, with results changing rapidly over recent years, which suggests e-mails are less popular with younger age groups. Note, however, that personalized advertising e-mails were acceptable for 79 percent of millennials, but around 44 percent of baby boomers said they found them "creepy"! Again, this statement depends on the reference sources used, because others suggest a higher proportion of baby boomers dislike personalized advertising—Gransnet surveys, for instance.

The ATTEST survey considers the question of which channels are the best to reach the target group with advertising and information about brands, and does provide some useful insights, as Table 11 shows.

Table 11 Best channels to reach the target group

	TV (%)	Social media (%)	Magazines (%)	None (%)
18–24	34	42	36	2
25–45, including millennials	34	40	27	2
46–64 mature	29	26	17	4
65–80+	28	13	12	11

Whereas TV is fairly similar in popularity across all age groups, the use of social media and even magazines may need closer analysis. For instance, the impact of advertising in magazines or social media platforms decreases significantly as age increases, although there is no indication of which magazines are the most/least popular with each age group.

The preferred social media channel is more significant than these broad statistics, given the wide difference in what each platform offers the user. In any event, social media is a crucial platform for those marketing existing brands or for anyone trying to break in with a new brand.

However, this survey covers a range of products and services. The research from Titan Travel, based specifically on the mature traveler, highlights how effective some TV coverage has been in relation to trips booked. For example, there have been several travel features recently on UK TV, with well-known celebrities taking part in trips to less familiar destinations such as Borneo and Uzbekistan. Both of these TV broadcasts were instantly followed by a surge in bookings for Uzbekistan, already identified as a potential new destination by various sources and tour operators, and for Titan Travel a 350 percent increase in bookings to Borneo.

Note that by the end of 2019, there has been a significant rise in the mature sectors registering for an Instagram account, around 20 percent but growing, suggesting that this may be related to increased demand for multigeneration holidays (Crisp 2019; Silver Travel Advisor 2020). Table 12 shows that Facebook continues to be the main route to reach customers irrespective of age group, although there are some differences with other forms of social media, and this is an ever-changing picture (Chart 3).

As with other surveys of this target group, a closer look at the use of social media gives some interesting insights. Facebook remains the main platform for those over 55 years old, 2018 seeing this as the largest sector joining

Table 12 Use of social media by age group

	Facebook (%)	Twitter (%)	WhatsApp (%)	LinkedIn (%)
18–24	64	38	30	17
25–45, including millennials	66	34	37	20
46–64 mature	61	28	28	11
65–80+ baby boomers	38	11	18	8

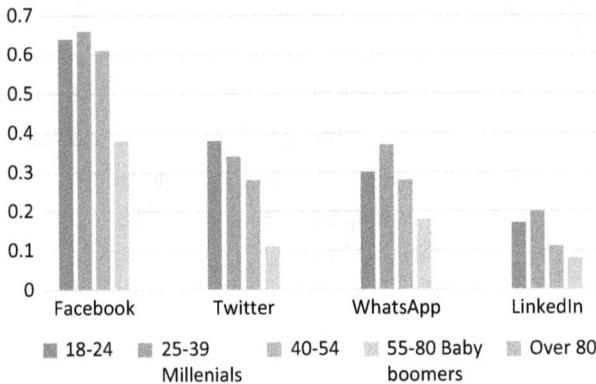

Chart 3 Preferred social media channels

Facebook, where more than 6.4 million users are aged over 50. In 2019, the Silver Travel Report noted that 67 percent of their mature travelers used Facebook, with a significant rise in numbers to 85 percent of respondents by the 2020 Report. Generally, around half that number have a Twitter account, around 31 percent in 2019, but also a growing trend by 2020.

Silver Travel Advisor has seen a real increase in the use of social media platforms even over a 12-month period. More significantly, in the 55–64 age group, the number of respondents not using the Internet dropped from 17 percent in 2019 to just 6 percent in 2020.

Now, in 2020, 64 percent use social media at least twice a day, 18 percent daily, and 40 percent post at least every other day when away—though note the implications for house insurance cover if it is found you advertised on Facebook that you were away from home for two weeks and were then burgled.

The 2019 Silver Travel Industry Report showed that in the 50- to 60-year-old group, 73 percent use their iPhone daily, 92 percent shop online, and 70 percent watch videos online. By the 2020 Industry Report, 85 percent use Facebook, and 82 percent of those use it daily, 55 percent use WhatsApp (free to send images), 24 percent use Twitter, and Instagram use has grown from 20 to 30 percent.

For this age group, the use of smartphones and iPads to browse websites is expanding so rapidly that by late 2020 Titan Travel, for example, expects their use to overtake the use of desktop computers. A more interesting factor is how many of their customers choose to speak to a travel advisor in person by phone, even when they have booked online or if they feel their booking is a bit more complicated than the standard format.

Wider research from Mintel (Titan Travel 2019–2020) suggests booking online is now the biggest route for the over-75 age group, just ahead of booking through an agent by phone. In the 65 to 74 years age group, 59 percent book online, as do 72 percent of those aged 55 to 64. Clearly, these channels are significant as part of any future strategy for reaching a specific mature traveler market.

There are other platforms that are growing in popularity, many aimed at the younger market (such as TikTok), and for the baby boomer category 36 percent said none of the social media channels were a preference. Feedback to the Attest survey suggests that the majority of customers prefer brands to contact them once a week or once a month rather than with a mix of different messages.

Based on the research evidence, we can summarize the various means available for getting the marketing message across to potential mature customers.

- E-mail is still the most popular route for receiving marketing messages.
- Social media platforms such as Facebook, Instagram, Twitter, and YouTube are growing rapidly.
- Competitions are mentioned by several survey respondents as a way to find out about brands and what they offer.
- Professional sites such as LinkedIn, aimed at those working in, or interested in, travel and tourism industry sectors.
- Various travel media and publications, magazines, e-zines, and the press (especially travel features or pull-out travel reports).

- TV shows featuring celebrities—but note that a large majority of the mature travel sector state they are not impressed by celebrity endorsement!
- The growing provision of special offer sites such as Travelzoo or Red Spotted Hanky and use of online comparison sites, stated by 23 percent of respondents.

There are still many in the older age brackets that prefer to book/arrange holidays in a face-to-face situation with a travel agent (just over a quarter of respondents to the Oddfellow survey) or online with a travel agent (31 percent of Travel Weekly survey respondents). However, Oddfellows also found that 21 percent of their members over 65 years old book online directly with a tour operator, and 22 percent book online for flights and accommodation separately (Oddfellows 2019).

There is a strong growing market for customers to book individual parts of their trip online rather than choose a package deal. The country profiles in the section "Where Do They Go?" show just how this varies according to nationality. Expedia is one of the major players in this area of decision-making and helping potential travelers choose the content of their trip, with an impressive score of 79 percent customer satisfaction in the U.S. market. Their global revenue is also an impressive $11.22 billion, $6.2 billion generated in the United States alone (ASTA 2020).

There are more players entering this field of booking separate elements for a vacation/trip, so competition to find and tempt customers to book is growing. Sites such as Trivago and Booking.com are rapidly expanding to offer a more comprehensive range of content to make it easier for travelers to choose in one place. At the time of writing, these three main channels to book are equally popular with UK travelers (Attest 2019).

Note that for the UK market 2019–2020, uncertainty about the impact of Brexit has been seen as a potential risk factor, with a shift to packages recognized by the ABTA, rather than booking separate elements, to ensure ATOL protection is there if needed. This is an element mentioned as a significant factor when choosing a holiday, alongside tour company collapse, global stability, and political unrest—54 percent cited this element of protection when asked to rank what they were looking for when choosing a trip.

In the United States, the mature traveler represented 64 percent of total travel packages booked through a travel agent, 4.5 million packages in 2017 increasing to 4.8 million packages in 2018 (USTA).

The role of travel agents has been shown to be as important now as in previous years, despite the assumption that everyone makes vacation and travel arrangements online. In the United States, for instance, travel agents have consistently increased revenue generated over the last decade, from $12.2 billion in 2010 to $15 billion in 2015 and estimated to be around $17.3 billion by the end of 2020 (US Travel Association 2019). Sales have been increasing year on year despite there being fewer travel agents, only 8 percent reporting a decrease in sales, and in the U.S. market 74 percent of travel agents state that they use mainly e-mail to attract new clients.

As we have seen in the discussions about options to book a trip, there is still an important role played by travel agents who are dealing with the mature traveler, particularly where more complex trips are planned.

PART 2

Country Profiles

Where Do They Go?

The following section summarizes where tourists travel to, based on country profiles (US Travel Association 2019) up to 2019. Clearly, this is just a sample of countries that have a significant body of tourists traveling overseas and is not a full global picture. However, it does make interesting reading when certain destinations appear in the top two to three positions irrespective of the home country. Note that it is mainly long-haul travel and not exclusively related to the 50+ age group, and the stated statistics may vary according to the source, method, and time of collection and analysis.

UK Travel Profile

There are more potential destinations identified in current trends later in this section, but it is useful to look more closely at the UK situation because this may well reflect that in other countries.

Overtourism is an issue in many parts of the UK, as in other parts of the world. London is a major destination, as you would expect—see Chart 4 breakdown of who visits London—with tourism representing a considerable source of income and contribution to GDP. Whereas U.S. tourists are the biggest group of visitors to London, others in the top ten list are from European states. Rural areas are also impacted directly by increasing numbers of tourists.

The waterways have opened up in recent years, particularly with improved riverside paths and canal towpaths, which often represent easier walking than coastal paths. Where the mature traveler is keen to enjoy a slower pace of travel, the journey being an integral part of the vacation, public transport links and connections are starting to improve in some areas to encourage more activities aimed at both domestic and overseas tourists.

Microbusinesses are growing in numbers in the UK, particularly in the area of food production, wine-making, brewing "craft" or small-batch

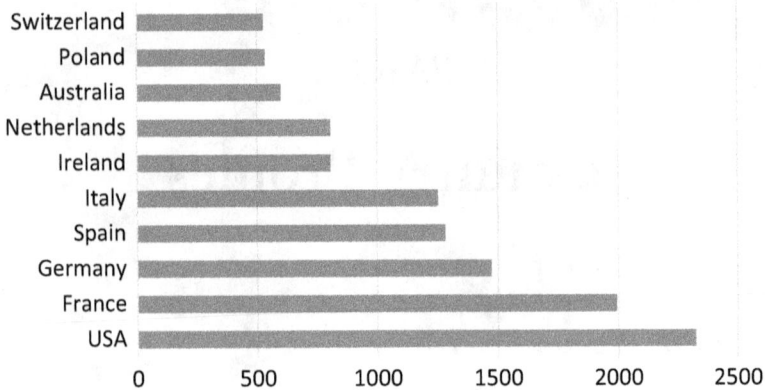

Chart 4 Visitors to London (Statista 2020)

beers, and spirit distilleries. Local farmers' markets also continue to be popular around the UK, bringing a wide range of fresh produce into more convenient town and village locations.

For the UK tourist, large-scale Christmas markets or traditional Victorian Fairs are a regular feature of promotions aimed at the target group, and British tourists represent a significant proportion of visitors to overseas markets, particularly those in Berlin and Hannover, Ostend, and Ghent. Such visits overseas generally involve coach, ferry, or cruise journeys.

As noted earlier, the staycation concept is becoming more appealing to an older market sector, often leading to shorter breaks but more frequent trips during the year. This can also be seen by the rapid growth in the popularity of Airbnb bookings, often just short-term breaks, with an over 600 percent increase in the number of lettings available by early 2020.

The domestic market in all countries has increased over recent years, but long term this is less clear in view of travel restrictions currently imposed in order to try and contain the rapid spread of COVID-19.

Top motivations stated by UK travelers for international travel include visiting cultural and historical attractions, experiencing the local lifestyle, relaxing on beaches and at the seaside, plus enjoying new and exciting dining and shopping experiences.

Table 13 gives a detailed picture of rise and fall in the popularity of long-haul destinations for UK travelers over the last five years. It shows that the top long-haul destinations for UK travelers stayed consistent and increased overall between 2015 and 2018, the only change being in the number of trips to the United States, which fell by 4.9 percent. Trips to India rose by almost a third and to Canada by over 10 percent, although numbers in millions are still considerably less than those traveling to the United States. Overall, numbers for long-haul travel did indeed rise over the year.

Table 13 Top long-haul destinations for UK travelers

Destination	2015 (in millions)	2018 (in millions)	% rise or fall in visits
United States	4,900	4,659	−4.9
UAE	1,500	1,582	+5.5
India	868	1,153	+32.9
Thailand	948	987	+4.2
Canada	716	791	+10.6
Overall trips taken	20,548	22,151	+7.8

Charts 5 and 6, with figures from the ONS (2018–2019) in the UK, show the number of visits made overseas had declined during the April to June period 2019 compared with the year earlier. This decline continued to the August figures in 2019. Reasons are varied, of course,

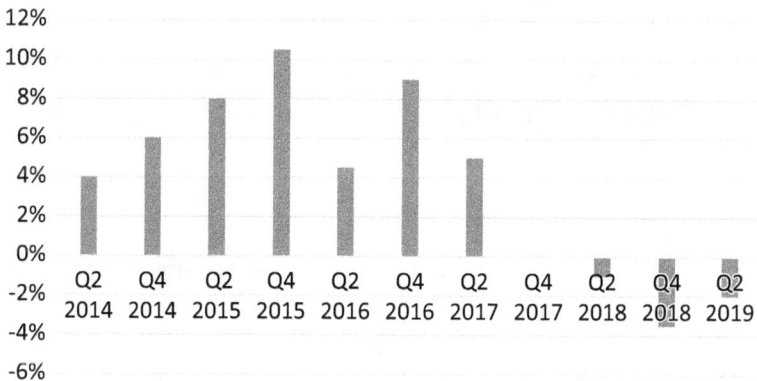

Chart 5 Number of visits overseas to June 2019 [ONS International Passenger survey]

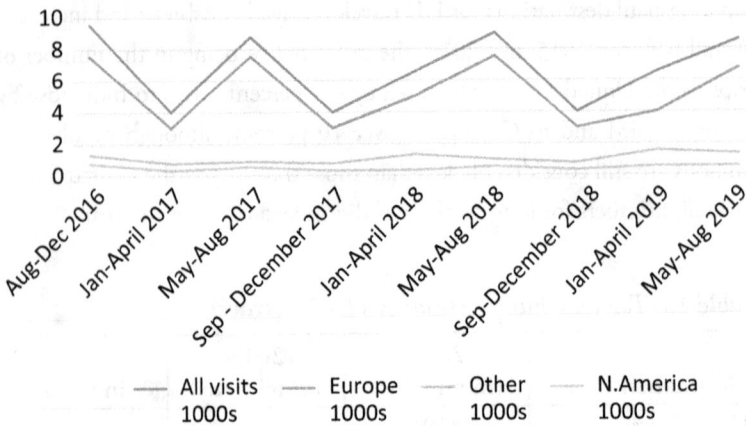

| All visits 1000s | Europe 1000s | Other 1000s | N.America 1000s |

Chart 6 Number of visits overseas to August 2019 [ONS International Passenger survey]

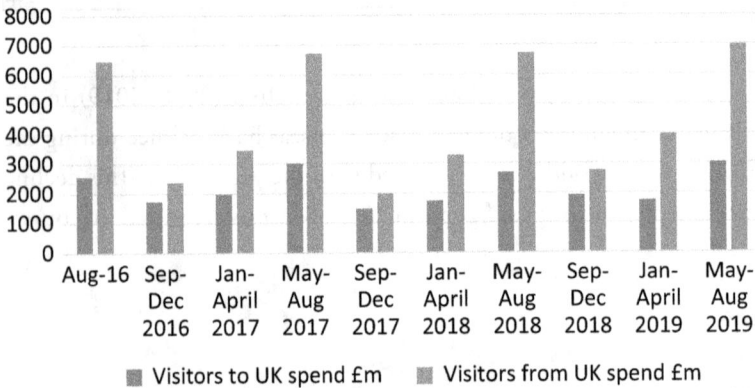

Visitors to UK spend £m   Visitors from UK spend £m

Chart 7 Patterns in spending [ONS International Passenger survey]

but uncertainty over the outcome of Brexit discussions is considered to be a factor. However, as Table 13 shows, visits to the United States were actually down on previous numbers, rather than to any other long-haul destinations, so it is not a simple case of reading the figures (Chart 7).

Despite fluctuations in destinations visited, spending by UK tourists traveling overseas followed a similar pattern between 2016 and 2019, apart from some increase in the first half of 2017. There is no indication of why except that the Brexit vote took place in 2016, so residents may have been keen to take their vacation while uncertain about how much travel plans would be affected in the future. This rise in spending also follows a similar pattern for overseas visitors to the UK during the same period. In addition, Chart 8 shows that spending abroad increased by 4 percent over the year to 2019.

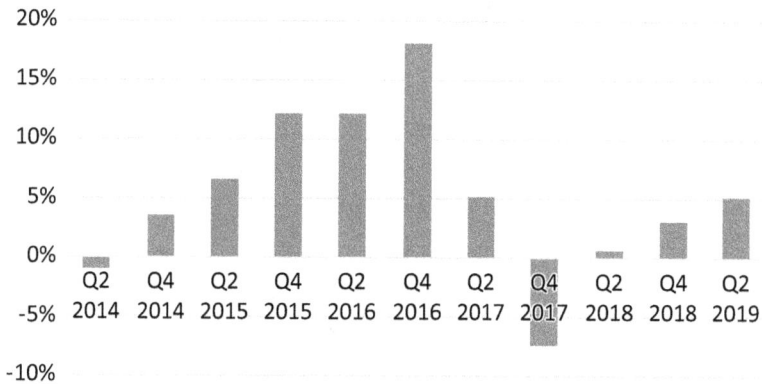

Chart 8 Increase in spending overseas [ONS International Passenger survey]

In 2019, the top 10 list of destinations for travelers from the UK [ONS/finder.com] were primarily in Europe (note that this is destinations overall rather than the earlier trips specifically defined as long-haul), with the United States ranking fourth in the list.

1. Spain 15.62 million
2. France 8.56m
3. Italy 4.16m
4. United States 3.47m
5. Ireland 3.42m
6. Portugal 2.87m

7. Germany 2.82m
8. Netherlands 2.72m
9. Poland 2.67m
10. Greece 2.34m

In addition, Trip Advisor published the following list of the most popular attractions booked through them in 2019 as mainland Europe, with just 3 out of 10 based in the United States.

- Colosseum, Rome (Rome also noted for luxury fashion goods shopping as well as exploring iconic architectural features (Condé Nast 2019))
- Louvre, Paris
- Vatican Museum, Rome
- Statue of Liberty, New York City
- Eiffel Tower, Paris
- Basilica of the Sagrada Familia, Barcelona
- French Quarter, New Orleans
- Anne Frank House, Amsterdam
- Skydeck Chicago, Willis Tower
- Piazza San Marco, Venice

Inbound tourist numbers to the UK continue to grow—see the ONS surveys above—and spending has stayed fairly consistent over previous years. As we note in a later section on the U.S. profile, U.S. spending in the UK is actually greater than UK spending in the United States.

Although the number of visitors from overseas remained fairly stable in 2019 compared with a year earlier (ONS 2018–2019; Statistics Poland/Statista 2019), spending did increase by 3 percent in just one-quarter of 2019; clearly, this is a positive sign. However, note that the ONS surveys, as well as some others that review the international travel and spending patterns, do not include breakdown by age group and are hence valuable inasmuch as they provide a useful picture of trends (Chart 9).

As 2020 is the year for the UK's withdrawal from the EU, it will be interesting to see how far these figures change in next year's statistics.

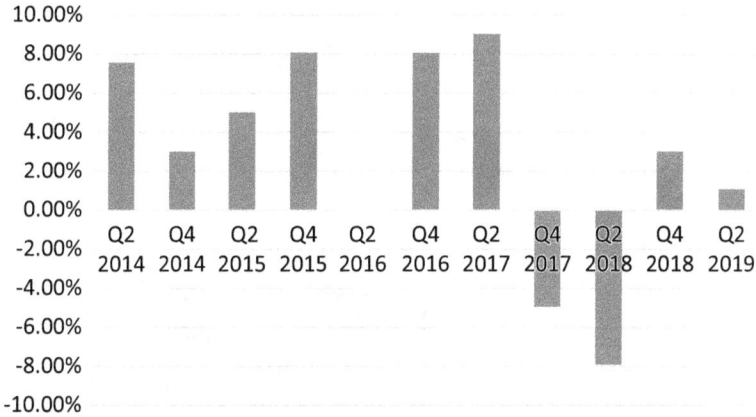

Chart 9 *Number of inbound visits to UK [ONS International Passenger survey]*

Even more crucial for our target sector is that more detailed analyses give a better picture of travel and spending according to age group or family basis.

U.S. Travel Profile

As we can see from other country profiles, travel to and from the United States is an important element of the worldwide travel market. Although this book is focused on the mature traveler over 50 to 55 years old, the overall picture of global travel has a direct impact on plans and future strategies for all those involved in the sector. In addition, research into the travel industry consistently demonstrates how important it is to get new customers and keep them loyal to the brand.

Both domestic and overseas travelers contributed almost $1.1 trillion to the GDP in 2018, so travel and tourism is a major element of the U.S. economy (US Travel Association 2019; USTOA 2018). The country profiles included here show there has been some fluctuation in the popularity of the United States as a travel destination in recent years. There has been some loss of business from countries that have traditionally seen the United States as a favorite destination, although California still remains popular – Image 4. Potential visitors are choosing to travel farther afield or try out new emerging travel markets.

Image 4 California [Photo by Viviana Rishe]

There are several different sources that identify the strength of inbound travel, generally agreeing with Table 14 from the National Travel and Tourism Office (NTTO) forecast based on actual figures in 2018 and on into the following five years (travel.trade.gov), plus feedback from USTA in 2019. Note that Canada and Mexico are not included as "Overseas" in the NTTO list, and in other sources it variously refers to the top inbound

Table 14 NTTO Forecast of inbound travel to the United States

Place	Country
1	Canada
2	Mexico
	Overseas
3	UK
4	Japan
5	China
6	South Korea
7	Brazil
8	Germany
9	France
10	India
11	Australia

nation as Canada or the UK followed by Mexico or Japan, so this explains these anomalies. Brazil and Germany are also interchangeable depending on which year's figures are used to decide their position.

The United States has long been one of the main long-haul tourist destinations for UK travelers, although this has declined over recent years, representing a total spend of around $16 billion and over 21 percent of U.S. exports. Visits to the United States have started to increase again from 2019, so it will be interesting to see how far it can develop its "competitive edge" (US Travel Association 2019) to attract still more visitors from the UK. However, around 27 percent of British travelers still consider the United States to be among the leading desired destinations.

Feedback from UK tourists gives some interesting insights into why they choose to visit the United States and what they are looking for or expecting from their visit. The most important content of the trip they are looking for is a chance to visit restaurants and sample the food, enjoy good accommodation, visit iconic attractions, and use local transport.

The primary purpose of the trip to the United States, which has changed little over the last two years, falls into the following main categories (Table 15).

Table 15 Primary purpose of trip to the United States from the UK

Primary trip purpose	
Vacation	65%
Visit friends and family	18%
Business trip	9%
Attend convention or trade shows	6%
Education	2%

The activities planned for the trip have also remained consistent over recent years, UK visitors stating the following range of experiences as a prerequisite for booking a visit (Table 16).

In 2018, the main destinations for UK travelers were Florida (28 percent), New York state (27 percent), and California (17 percent), with around 12 percent saying this was the first time they had been to the United States. (Table 17).

Table 16 *Planned activities during visit to the United States*

Planned activities	
Shopping	85%
Sightseeing	82%
Visits to parks and monuments	38%
Visits to historical locations	31%
Fine dining	30%

Table 17 *Top cities visited in the United States*

City visited	
New York	27%
Orlando	19%
Las Vegas	10%
Los Angeles	9%
San Francisco	8%

Visitors from the UK were the biggest group of tourists to visit New York City (Statista 2020) in 2018, closely followed by those from China and Canada—see Chart 12.

While UK travelers to the United States say they find the people friendly and adventurous, with a diverse mix, there are also some specific deterrents to booking a visit. The following list shows that some of these have remained consistent, but there are some further points raised in the 2019 feedback compared with a year earlier (Table 18).

Table 18 *Deterrents stopping UK tourists visiting the United States*

Deterrent	2019 (%)	2018 (%)
Airfare too expensive	34	
United States too expensive	24	44
Concern for personal safety	18	16
Strict security policies	16	
Better destinations exist	15	15
Not enough vacation time available	15	14

The cost is clearly seen as an issue, but note that the airfare has been picked out as a specific deterrent for UK travelers, and, overall, the United States is seen as an expensive destination. For the UK, there has been some uncertainty since the Brexit referendum in 2016, and the value of the pound sterling against other currencies, including the U.S. dollar, has had an impact on spending. For instance, the pound had been depreciating against the U.S. dollar for some years, falling by a further 13 percent by the end of 2018. It will be interesting to see how much the rates change from 2020 onwards as the UK has now left the EU. Note the later reference to the impact of exchange rates when deciding where to go in the future.

Around 20 percent of UK tourists use social media to plan and book their trip, with 17 percent opting for a prepaid package deal that includes all their preferred activities, so still a large percentage prefer to book individual parts of their trip separately. On average, they will spend nine nights in the United States, quite a short stay compared with other nationalities, but trips to New York City, for instance, are generally viewed as a short break either for shopping or to enjoy a specific event.

Summary of Main Features of Inbound Travel from Country Profiles

The following examples summarize significant features about travel to the United States from a selection of countries that see it as a key destination.

The U.S. share of long-haul travel from the UK declined from 24 percent in 2015 to 21 percent in 2018, although numbers have started to increase again from 2019. In 2018, there were 2.7 million visitors from the UK, spending an average $4,241 per person. By 2018, however, visits from the United States to the UK increased, representing a bigger spend by them at $16.7 billion.

Poland is one of the fastest-growing inbound travel markets, with visits by Polish tourists increasing year on year by around 5 percent for five consecutive years. In fact, the U.S travel industry predicts that visitor numbers from Poland are likely to continue to increase, rising by 233,000 over the next three years.

The 3 million Chinese visitors in 2018 represent 7.5 percent of inbound travel to the United States from overseas. The differences between the Chinese traveler to the United States and other nationals seem to be accounted for by the greater importance of education and business as the primary purpose, together representing around a third of all trips. Despite this as the stated reason behind the trip, the main activities once there are shopping (86 percent), sightseeing (79 percent), visiting museums and national monuments around 40 percent each.

There were 2.1 million German visitors in 2018, representing 5.2 percent of inbound travelers, although this means they have dropped from their position in the previous year. While the number of German visits to the United States has declined overall since 2016, and is expected to stay flat during 2019, there is some suggestion that it may grow a little during 2020. (US Travel Association 2019). Table 19 shows that the main activities for German visitors during their stay have changed little since 2017.

Table 19 Main activities by German tourists visiting the United States

Activities during their stay in the United States	2018 (%)	2017 (%)
Shopping	84	83
Sightseeing	80	82
Visits to national parks and monuments	41	45
Visiting small towns	40	41
Historical locations	36	36

German visitors to the United States went mainly to New York (31 percent) and California (24 percent) and rated sixth in the number of tourists visiting New York City (see Chart 10). A particular attraction that appealed to the German traveler was stated as an opportunity to "experience nature," so this is an important element of content before making a final choice of destination. On average, a German tourist will stay for 11 nights in the United States, mainly for a vacation (58 percent), and 12 percent saw it as one of the top bucket list destinations. The primary reason for visiting has changed little between 2017 and 2018, according to feedback from travel agencies in the United States (Table 20).

The impressions they have of a visit to the United States is that it is a diverse mix of people, who are adventurous and forward-thinking and friendly. The main activities they take part in are typical of tourists from other countries and, again, have varied little between 2017 and 2018. Shopping in the United States consistently appears near the top of the list of activities irrespective of currency exchange rate difficulties.

Table 20 Primary reason for trip to the United States from Germany

Primary reason for trip	2018 (%)	2017 (%)
Vacation	58	58
To visit friends and relatives	19	18
Business	14	13
Convention or trade show	5	6
Education	3	3
Other	1	2

Note that more U.S. residents visited Germany (3 million) than German tourists visited the United States (2.1 million) in 2019, and German tourists spent more money on their trip than U.S. citizens did when visiting Germany.

Japan is the second largest inbound market, with 3.5 million visitors in 2018, a fall from earlier years but now showing signs of increasing from 2019. The same number of Japanese travelers visited the United States in 2018 as all the countries of Western Europe, so the United States is by far the top destination for Japanese travelers. 46 percent visited Hawaii, 16 percent California, and 8 percent New York.

Although visits to the United States are continuing to grow year on year, there are still some things that act as a deterrent to Japanese tourists. These include the cost of airfare and the vacation being too expensive, stated by 46 percent in 2019, and 30 percent of potential visitors not having enough holiday time available from work, generally a higher proportion than travelers from other countries. The primary purpose of their trip is stated as vacation by 71 percent of visitors and business by 13 percent, generally spending an average of four nights in the United States. As with other visitors to the United States, sightseeing, shopping, and guided tours are high on the list of activities they participate in, connecting with nature appearing high on the list of what they are looking for when considering booking a trip.

Australia is in the 9th position (11th if you include Canada and Mexico) for inbound tourist numbers, being the highest spending visitors at $6,000 on average. Australians spend on average 14 nights when traveling to the United States, 45 percent visiting California, 27 percent visiting Hawaii, 23 percent visiting New York, and 31 percent visiting Los Angeles.

Australian tourists ranked 6th in the number of visitors to New York City, and the United States represents a 7 percent share of outbound travel from Australia. The primary purpose of a trip to the United States is vacation or visiting friends and relations. The main content they look for when making their final choice of destination is access to urban attractions, shopping, beaches, cultural and historical attractions and experiencing the local lifestyle, so little has changed year on year (Table 21).

Table 21 *Activities during a visit to United States by Australian tourists*

Activities during visit	2018 (%)	2017 (%)
Shopping	91	92
Sightseeing	91	91
National parks and monuments	54	56
Guided tours	49	50
Visiting small towns	44	43
Historical locations	42	45
Art gallery and museums	38	40

In feedback to tour operators, a third of potential tourists from Australia cited poor exchange rates as a deterrent to booking a trip. However, 34 percent still say the United States is among the leading desired destinations, including a visit to New York City – Chart 10.

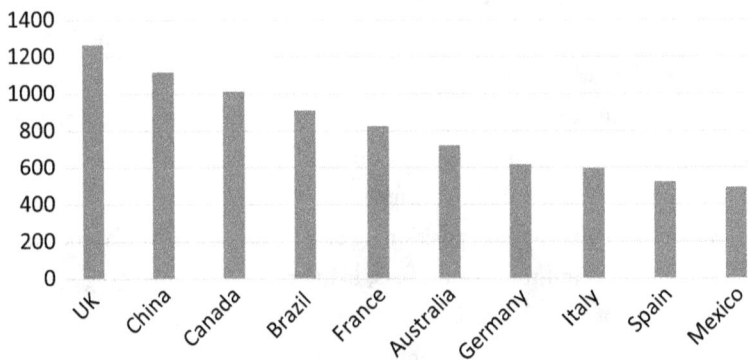

Chart 10 *Tourists visiting New York City 2018*

Travel from India represents $15.8 billion and is in the eighth position for inbound tourists, with 1.38 million visitors. There is steady growth in the number of visitors from India. For trips to the United States, travelers from India are among the highest spenders, compared with other nationals visiting, and the average length of a stay is 15 nights. 30 percent of travelers from India visited California, 29 percent New York, and 12 percent Texas. The primary purpose of their visit to the United States tends to be something other than vacation, and India is second only to China in the number of nationals studying there. Despite the focus on business as a primary purpose of the visit, shopping and sightseeing are still high on the list of activities, with activities changing little from the previous year (Table 22).

Table 22 Primary purpose of visit to United States from India

Primary purpose of visit to United States	2019 (%)	2018 (%)
Business	36	39
Visit friends and family	31	31
Vacation	15	14
Attend a trade show	12	9
Education	6	6

If we look at the U.S. market and visitors from India, the average age of those booking is younger than from any other inbound tourist country at 39 years. However, there are often larger family groups traveling together with extended family, so the mature market is still there (though potentially reduced).

Visits from Mexican tourists grew by 3.9 percent in 2018, accounting for 23 percent of international visits, with 18.5 million overnight stays. In 2018, the United States, as a destination, represented 83 percent of outbound travel from Mexico. For travel to the United States, Mexico is actually the second largest inbound market, after Canada, the majority of visitors crossing the border by land and only 15 percent by air (although this increased by 9.6 percent in 2018). 21 percent of travelers from Mexico visited California, 18 percent visited Texas, and 18 percent Florida. By the beginning of 2020, with discussions about installing a physical wall between the United States and Mexico, it is not clear what impact this will have on visitor numbers.

Canada is the highest inbound travel sector, with 21.5 million stays in 2018 excluding day trips, still a significant number but declining from previous years. Two-thirds of Canadians have visited the United States in the last five years, and 39 percent have stated they would be interested in visiting in the next two years. Figures also suggest that over half the number of trips made by Canadian tourists were to the United States.

Top Destinations and Trends Identified by U.S. Travel Agents

The leading international destinations in 2017, according to the volume of sales by tour operator members of USTA, were Mexico, Italy, Germany, France, United Kingdom, Netherlands, Spain, Ireland, Switzerland, and Australia.

Italy was named the most popular destination for U.S. travelers in 2019. The top 10 "hot" destinations for 2020 also included Iceland, which ranked second, followed by Japan, Vietnam, Australia, France, Spain, Colombia, Cambodia, and Portugal.

Travel agents identified the top destination categories for U.S. travelers in 2019 as follows, noting the significant increase in plans to visit Europe (Table 23).

Table 23 Destination categories booked through travel agents for 2019

Destinations booked through U.S. travel agents	
Europe	41%
The Caribbean	20%
Asia and the Middle East	11%
South America and Central America	22%
Other	6%

Members of USTOA identified their top 10 off-the-beaten-path or emerging destinations that they see gaining popularity in 2019. Iceland ranked first, Cambodia second, followed by Croatia, Colombia, Vietnam, Portugal, Bhutan, Bolivia, Myanmar, and Ethiopia, adding up to a very wide range of potential destinations that appear to support the need for action on "overtourism".

There was some interesting feedback concerning the American perception of travel to India. Only 4 percent said they would like to visit India for the spring break, presumably owing to concerns about distance and cost, although 7 percent would consider a vacation in India. A greater number, at 24 percent, said their perception of India as an attractive travel destination had improved, so the picture is not quite so bleak.

The World demographic profile in Table 1 shows the U.S. population breakdown of around 70 percent under 55 years old and 30 percent aged over 55, and hence a significant mature sector in actual numbers. USTA found that 51 percent of the U.S. population classed as baby boomers preferred to look for domestic destinations within the United States, thus contributing to the 80 percent domestic travel spending. In the travel and tourism industries, nearly half (48 percent) of customers arranging some form of travel through them (USTOA 2018) are aged 51 to 70, only 20 percent of customers aged 36 to 50.

There are some interesting differences in popularity of domestic destinations between 2017 and 2018, so it would be particularly interesting to see how these changed for 2019–2020 (Table 24).

Table 24 Top domestic destinations in U.S 2017–2018 (based on sales)

Destinations 2017	Destinations 2018
California	Alaskan cruise
Hawaii	Orlando
New York	Las Vegas
Florida	New York City
Nevada	Honolulu
Arizona	Hawaiian cruise
Alaska	Miami
Colorado	Washington, DC
U.S. Virgin Islands	Los Angeles

In terms of the average cost of a week's summer vacation, American tourists spend more than other nationals (irrespective of where they visit), at $1692.93, closely followed by Switzerland, Germany, and the UK spend of $1407.26 (Chart 11, Statista 2020).

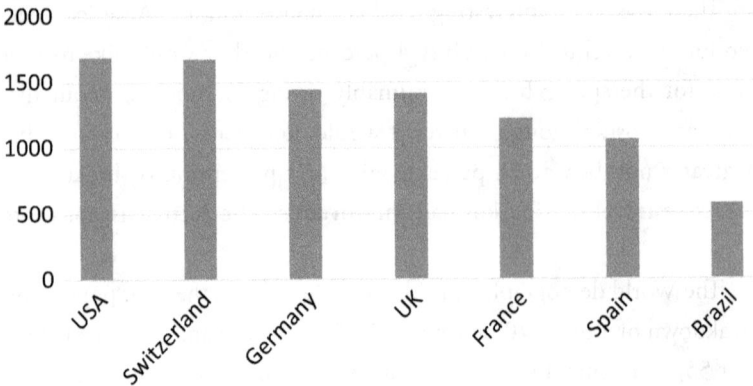

Chart 11 Cost per week for summer holiday/vacation

The United States is one of the biggest spenders on business travel, at $292.29 billion, a growth of 6 percent, and 74 percent plan their business trip via the Internet.

The U.S. Tour Operators Association (USTOA) provided a range of travel and tourism packages to 9.8 million travelers in 2018. They noted in a recent member survey that nearly half of their customers, 48 percent, were aged over 51 and that European destinations were increasingly being booked by U.S. travelers.

Canada Travel Profile

As with some of the other country profiles, Canada is made up of a diverse business and social background, with a $1.8-trillion economy and a population of 37.5 million (US Travel Association 2019). It too has a significant aging population, with nearly a third aged over 55 and almost double the world demographic picture with 18.10 percent aged over 65.

Around 90 percent of the population lives within 100 miles of the Canada/U.S. border, with 21.5 million visits to the United States in 2018, not including day trips, so the United States remains at the top of the list of preferred destinations for Canadian tourists. There is some evidence that the mature traveler prefers to visit nearby United States, particularly the south (Florida) for the sun, rather than travel farther afield worldwide.

The majority of Canadians (56 percent) travel to the United States overland, with 44 percent arriving by plane. Once they arrive, air travel is preferred, although 51 percent also said they likely to drive between cities. Visiting friends and family is one of the main reasons they choose to visit, but restaurants and food always appear high on the list of things they are looking for.

The top reason for not visiting the United States is the currency exchange rate, which makes it expensive for Canadian tourists, along with concerns about national politics and personal safety—often quoted as concerns by travelers generally but not usually as the main criteria. However, there have been attempts to overcome the problem of currency fluctuations along some of the border states, including offering to accept the same number of Canadian dollars for the prices stated in U.S. dollars.

Canada is in the third position for the number of tourists that visited New York City. The number of visits has been declining as trips to other destinations have increased by 7 percent, overall, and trips to some destinations such as Italy by significant numbers (Table 25).

Table 25 Increase in share of visits to top five destinations from Canada 2013–2018 (USTA)

Destination	% share 2013	% share 2018
United States	64	54.9
Mexico	4.3	5.2
Cuba	3	3.6
France	2.7	2.8
Italy	1.6	2.6

Although these figures represent the share of overall outbound travel, the picture looks different in terms of the actual number of visitors to destinations. Note also that there is a difference in the way outbound travel is defined between Canada, the United States, and Mexico in relation to classification as "long-haul." For example, Table 26 identifies the increase in travel from Canada to long-haul destinations with no mention of the United States.

Table 26 Increase in number of visitors to long-haul destinations from Canada

Long-haul outbound destinations	% increase
Italy	+75
Cuba	+29
Mexico	+28
Dominican Republic	+28
China	+24
UK	+16
France	+11

Image 5 Blue lake in Canada [Photo by Johny Goerend]

There are many reasons for increased travel to certain destinations that are not necessarily straightforward, of course, whether it is improved flight routes, easier access to the country (such as Cuba), or increased levels of disposable income. It is also likely that increased use of online platforms to search for and book travel, and better marketing use of these platforms, has a direct impact on numbers. These issues are discussed in later chapters.

Mexico Travel Profile

Mexico has been included in this section because it appears frequently on lists of destinations visitors have traveled or would travel to, and they are a growing market for future tourist activity. There were 41 million inbound travelers to Mexico in 2018, spending $22.4 billion and making it the seventh largest global market. Even though this is such a considerable source of income for the country, there has been a shift away from the provision of a Mexico Tourism Board (having closed many of its offices overseas) to relying on a range of other private organizations for marketing and promotion to potential travelers. It remains to be seen (in 2020) how this will affect tourist numbers, particularly given the perceived concerns about crime and personal safety, but it presents a considerable opportunity for tour operators and travel agents worldwide to develop strategies to increase tourist visits to Mexico.

It is a growing economy, perhaps slowing down a little from 2019, with a diverse offering to global markets. They have more free trade agreements arranged, with 46 countries, than any other nation.

From a mature travel perspective, they have a younger demographic profile, with the 55+ age group at just 15.77 percent, a similar profile to that of India. For those who do travel from Mexico, 37 percent use social media to help them plan a trip, but only 6 percent choose a package deal, preferring to arrange the content of the visit themselves.

Travelers are looking mainly for trips to theme parks, having family fun with good hotels and restaurants. The primary purpose stated for the trip is vacation, then visiting family and friends, which has changed little from the previous year. Those who travel to the United States by air, suggested to be those with more disposable income, stay an average of six nights (Table 27).

Table 27 Primary purpose of trip to United States from Mexico

Primary purpose of trip	2018 (%)	2017 (%)
Vacation	53	50
Visiting friends and family	21	23
Business	17	16
Visit to a convention or trade show	5	7
Education	3	2
Other	1	2

Although shopping (83 percent) and sightseeing (65 percent) remain the most popular activities—Mexican visitors ranking 10th in the number of tourists visiting New York City—experiencing fine dining is listed by around a fifth of visitors from Mexico.

Of more significance for the U.S. travel market is the outline of things that deter Mexican tourists from visiting the United States (Table 28).

Table 28 *Things that deter tourists from Mexico visiting United States*

Deterrents from visiting United States	2018 (%)	2017 (%)
Poor currency exchange rates	32	44
Unhappy about U.S. politics	29	34
Too expensive	26	35
Security policies	26	
Cost of airfare	22	
Don't feel welcome in the United States	22	24
Personal safety	20	22

Although the later year includes more criteria than in 2017, the concerns about not feeling welcome and personal safety still amount to over 40 percent of respondents. The cost of airfare plus the overall cost of a visit being "too expensive" is identified by 48 percent of potential visitors, more than the 35 percent stated the previous year.

Australia Travel Profile

Since the 1980s, Australia has been developing in the context of business, economy, and real growth in GDP to become one of the most diverse economies in the world. It has a wealth of natural resources to build on and even with the occasional slowing down of perceived growth, still continues to move forward. From a tourism perspective, the depreciation of the Australian dollar against the U.S. dollar (2012–2015) did make travel to the United States particularly expensive, but 1.4 million visitors still found the United States an attractive destination.

Overall, visits overseas have increased by 18 percent over the last five years.

The top five destinations, along with share in numbers of tourists visiting these destinations since 2015, are shown in Tables 29 and 30, with Indonesia and New Zealand ranked more highly than the United States as a preferred destination.

Guided tours are an important part of the package they are looking for and a significant proportion of visitors, 27 percent, use social media

Table 29 Most popular destinations and share of
outbound tourism from Australia 2015–2018

Popular destinations for Australian tourists	Increase/decrease 2015–2018 (%)
Indonesia	+60
France	+34
New Zealand	+13
Italy	+13
United States	−6
UK	−4

Source: Tourism Economics and U.S. Department of Commerce (for U.S. arrivals)

Table 30 Share of number of outbound tourists from Australia

Destination	2015% share	2018% share	Visits in millions
Indonesia	7	9.4	1.8
New Zealand	8.4	8	1.5
United States	9.2	7.3	1.4
UK	6.6	5.3	1.0
Italy	5.1	4.9	0.9
Total outbound travel numbers			18.7

to help plan a trip, with 9 to 10 percent opting for a package deal rather than booking individual elements.

Japan Travel Profile

As a highly developed diverse economy, worth $4.9 trillion, Japan is a big contributor to the U.S. economy through travel and tourism as the top destination for Japanese travelers, 3.5 million visiting the United States in 2018—almost the same number that visited the whole of Western Europe in the same period.

The main content they are looking for from a trip is dining out, visiting cultural and historical attractions, shopping, and experiencing the local lifestyle. Whereas 16 percent use social media to plan the trip, almost half (46 percent) prefer to book a complete package online or with a travel agent.

It is clear from Table 31 that many long-haul destinations are being seen less favorably than in previous years, but these figures relate to travel data up to 2018. It remains to be seen how far numbers have increased by the end of 2020 and which countries join or leave the list of most popular destinations.

Table 31 *Top five long-haul destinations for Japanese travelers*

Destination	Visitors in millions 2015	Visitors in millions 2018	% change +/−
United States	3.88	3.49	−7.9
Germany	0.65	0.61	−5.3
France	0.68	0.56	−17
Spain	0.61	0.55	−9.3
Australia	0.34	0.47	+37
Total long-haul travel	9.8	9.6	−1.8

The demographic profile for Japan presents some real concerns at every level in society. It is an aging population with 30,000 centenarians (Silver Travel Advisor 2020), although their fitness levels are generally considered to be impressive for these age groups.

33 percent of the population are over 60

28 percent are over 65

20 percent are over 70.

Tourist visits to Japan have been increasing steadily over the last 10 years, as you can see from Chart 12, so inbound tourism has a lot of potential to develop further.

The number of incoming tourists has risen from 6.22 million in 2011 to 28.9 million in 2017 and spending by visitors is almost five times greater in that period, going from 0.81 to 4.42 thousand Japanese yen. More recent events, such as hosting World Cup sports competitions, have made an even greater impact on income from tourism. The example later in the book shows how effective their strategy has been in attracting new tourists.

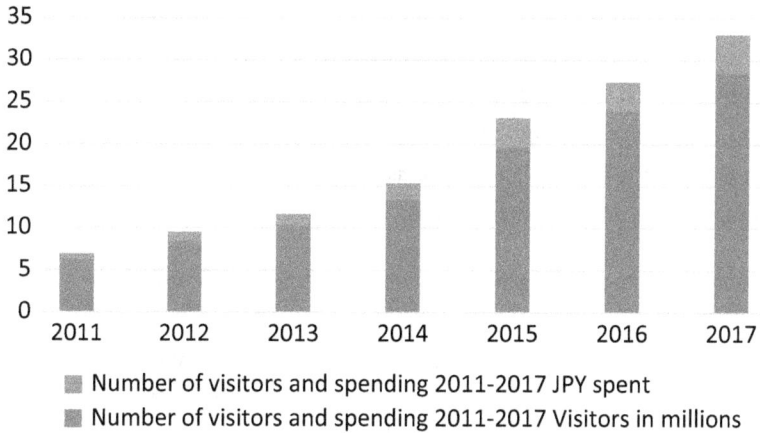

Chart 12 *Increase in inbound tourist numbers and spend*

At the beginning of 2020, the impact of the coronavirus in the Far East is rapidly bringing tourism and travel to an unprecedented low as governments and medical professions try to halt its spread. Unfortunately, long-haul travel, including flights and cruise ships, is particularly at risk because of the close proximity of travelers over long journey times—a critical risk for all operators and providers of services to the travel industry.

China travel profile

There is no doubt that China is an important player when considering tourism, both inbound and outgoing, with a growing economy ($13.6 trillion 2019) and a population of 1.4 billion. As with other countries globally, they are experiencing a growth in the older sectors of the community alongside a long-term tradition of limited birth rates. The "world demographics" table, at the beginning of the book, clearly shows how different their demographic profile is compared with many other major economies of the world. However, other factors such as the number of families who choose to travel with multigeneration members will have an impact on strategies chosen to target mature Chinese travelers.

There is an increase in the number of Chinese nationals who hold a passport and travel to long-haul destinations, growing by 4.3 percent overall in 2018, with a spread of countries visited. Table 32 shows the top five choices of long-haul destination, with a decline in the number of visits to the United States, but, as you can see, this still only represents around half of the countries visited.

Table 32 Top five long-haul destinations for Chinese travelers 2015–2018

Destination	2015 share (%)	2018 share (%)	Number of travelers in 2018 in millions
United States	15.3	12.9	3.0
France	12.8	9.2	2.1
Russia	6.7	9	2.1
Germany	8.1	6.9	1.6
Australia	6	6.2	1.4
Other	51.1	55.8	12.9
Total long-haul travel			23.1

The four main destinations that did grow in popularity included those listed in Table 33.

Table 33 Travel destinations and % increase in number of visitors from China 2018

Travel destinations and % increase	
UAE	+10.7%
Australia	+5.5%
Switzerland	+5.3%
Germany	+2.5%

When planning a trip, 35 percent of Chinese travelers use social media, and 18 percent choose a package deal that includes nature experiences, ecotourism, culture, and history as important elements of the content of trips. When visiting the United States, the activities they take part in have changed a little between 2017 and 2018, although the primary purpose of the trip is consistent, with 33 to 34 percent as a vacation and around a quarter to visit friends and family.

Until early 2020, there were major issues facing the travel and tourism industries and China as a destination. There is widespread concern for health, personal safety of Chinese nationals visiting outside their country, and restrictions and cancellations of flights and travel packages. Even before the coronavirus outbreak currently associated with China, there was a fall in tourist activity in Hong Kong and widespread political unrest, which does not help when trying to promote the country as a potential destination for mature travelers (Chart 13, statista.com/Hong Kong Tourist Board).

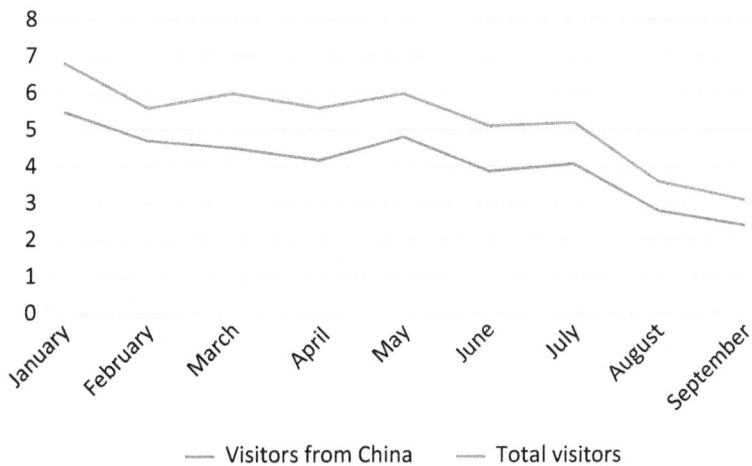

Chart 13 *Decline in number of tourists visiting Hong Kong 2019*

India Travel Profile

India is seen as one of the fastest-growing travel markets in the world, with a population of 1.4 billion, which is likely to grow to be the world's largest population within the next decade, and an estimated $2.7-trillion economy (US Travel Association 2019). The biggest shift since the 1950s has been from a primarily agricultural economy to one where this is now closer to 15 percent, industry sectors around 33 percent, and service sector at 52 percent.

Travel and tourism have been a key element of the Indian economy, contributing $208.9 billion in 2016 and making India the second highest contributor in Asia-Pacific, second only to China and followed by

Thailand. The numbers of Indian nationals traveling overseas as tourists is clearly significant, growing by 31 percent between 2015 and 2018, and 9.3 percent in just one year to 2018.

The number of visits by Indian tourists to many destinations has risen significantly since 2018 and continues to grow at an impressive rate (Table 34).

Table 34 Rise in tourist numbers outbound from India to 2018

Destinations for outbound tourists	Number of tourists (in millions)	% rise
UAE	2.58	30
Thailand	1.6	49
Saudi Arabia	1.44	5.5
United States	1.38	20
Bahrain	1.04	45.4
Overall increase in outbound travel		31.1

There are many factors that influence growth in tourism including the search for new experiences such as a Riverboat trip (Image 6). For India, an important change was the introduction of an easier visa application procedure and an increase in the number of countries that could apply for an e-visa. Over five years this grew from just 11 to 161 in 2018, with the UK and the United States being the top two countries to use this new system. As you can see, this has led to a clear increase in revenue from tourist spending (Chart 14, Statista 2020).

Image 6 Riverboat in India [Photo by Kyran Low]

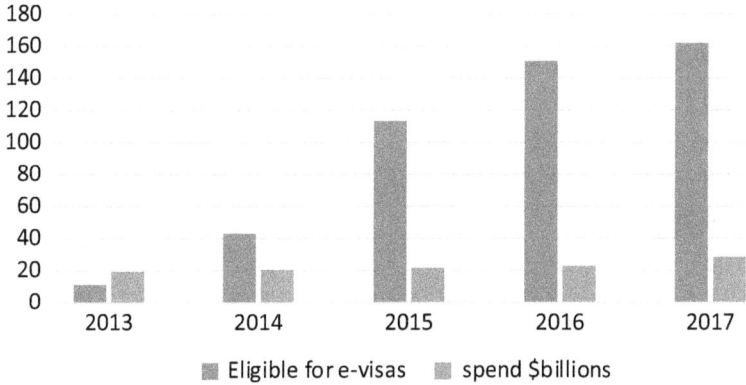

Chart 14 *Effect of new visa procedures for travel to India*

Although visitor numbers have continued to grow, there has also been a clear dip in numbers around 2012–2013, when personal safety became a serious concern with news of gang rape incidents escalating (Chart 15).

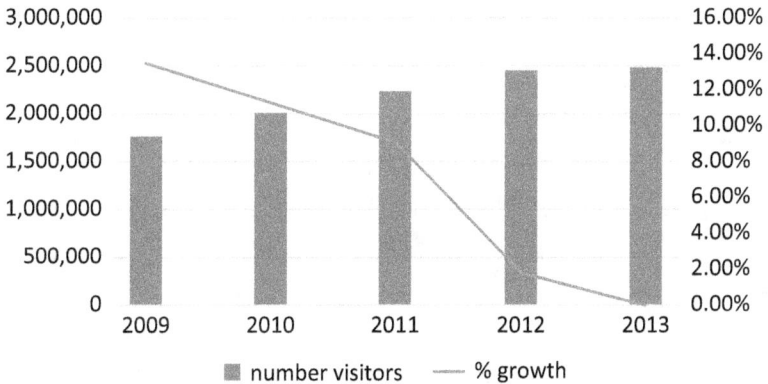

Chart 15 *Impact of safety concerns for tourists to India 2013*

As we are looking at the mature travel market, India presents some interesting issues for tour operators and travel providers. The demographic profile is somewhat different from the other major countries we have looked at so far. More than half the population in India is under 30 years old, with less than a quarter aged 45+. Although there are always exceptions, of course, the life expectancy in India is 68 years for men and 70 years for women.

Forty-three percent of visitors to the United States from India, for example, use social media to help plan a trip, and 12 percent choose a package deal. As with other countries, the cost of the trip is a deterrent to more than half of potential customers, and, in addition, poor exchange rates are cited as a deterrent by more than a quarter of respondents.

Germany Travel Profile

With a population of around 82 million, Germany ranks 17th in population globally and 19th based on GDP (just behind Hong Kong and just ahead of Belgium), so it is, clearly, a significant market in relation to travel and tourism. As in Japan and many other countries worldwide, the population growth rate has slowed, and the number of older people in society is growing (Table 35).

Table 35 Top long-haul destinations for German tourists 2015–2018 (US Travel Association 2019)

Destination	Visits in millions 2015	Visits in millions 2018	% change in number of visits
United States	2,285	2,062	−9.7
Egypt	1,021	1,638	+60.5
Thailand	762	890	+16.8
UAE	644	752	+16.7
China	623	655	+5
Total long-haul travel	11,606	13,542	+16.7

Potential long-haul destinations from Germany have shown a significant increase over a three-year period of around 17 percent, the United States still retaining the largest share, although reduced from previous years. For instance, travel from Germany to Egypt increased by a substantial 60.5 percent, to Thailand and to UAE by almost 17 percent each, and to China by 5 percent.

Only around 10 percent of potential German tourists used social media to help with decision-making, and just 9 percent opted for a package deal. Hence, it appears that more German tourists are looking for the individual parts that make up a trip, such as with Expedia, rather than a full package deal (expedia.com 2020).

Clearly, Germany remains a substantial market for overseas travel and, just as important, for travel within Europe and into neighboring countries (see notes on Poland).

Poland Travel Profile

A profile of Poland has been included here because it represents a later arrival to the EU, and it is seen as an increasingly significant player in global travel, both inbound and as a target market for other destinations.

Since Poland became a member of the EU, its travel and tourism sectors have increased significantly. This is partly because of its EU membership, and therefore accessibility, but also because of its competitive prices and a growing provision of health, wellness, and spa facilities. Just as critical for the Polish travel market has been its admission into the Visa Waiver Program in 2019 and therefore potential increase in travel to the United States.

Image 7 Ship moored on river in Poland [Photo by Anna Gru]

In 2018, there were 19.6 million tourists visiting Poland and 66.3 million day-visitors, around one-third aged over 55 (stat.gov.pl). In total, including Polish and overseas tourists, there were 34 million arrivals at tourist overnight accommodation in 2018. The majority of visitors are from neighboring Germany, 34 percent of these as tourists staying more than one night and over 40 percent just for the day. Most tourists stay in hotels, motels, or boarding houses. Overnight stays in the three main cities of Warszawa, Krakow, and Kolobrzeski amounted to 6.4 million, 5.6 million, and 5.1 million, respectively.

Of foreign tourists visiting during the main July and August period, 19 percent stayed at coastal resorts, 6 percent in mountain areas, but the bulk, 75 percent, stayed in other parts of Poland. Visitors to Poland are primarily from nearby or European countries, with just a few from farther afield, including the United States and Israel (Table 36).

Table 36 Nationality of visitors to Poland 2018

Visitors to Poland 2018	% (approx.)
Germany	26
France, Spain, and Italy	10
UK	8
Ukraine	7
Sweden and Norway	5
United States	5
Russia	4
Israel	3.5
Latvia	2.5
Other	24

In 2018, 61.9 percent of Polish residents made at least one tourist trip, the average being 3 trips per year, which was a 10.5 percent increase on the number of trips made in 2017. Two million outbound trips in 2018 were to Germany. Long-haul destinations for Polish travelers have changed in 2018 compared with 2017, and this is likely to change still further in 2019 (Table 37, figures available only up to 2018 on stat.gov .pl at the time of writing).

Table 37 Top long-haul destinations from Poland and numbers of tourists

Long-haul destinations	2018	2017
Egypt	220,000	150,000
United States	211,000	200,000
China	90,000	85,000
Canada	48,000	50,000
Morocco	46,000	52,000
Cuba	40,000	40,000

Although the number of trips to Morocco and Canada have reduced, visits to China, the United States, and Egypt have shown a significant increase—an all-time high for visits to the United States.

Clearly, Poland is an emerging destination for travelers, with the potential to increase its inbound tourist numbers significantly as it develops wider recognition as an attractive place to visit. It also has a growing base of potential tourists looking for other destinations to visit as their outbound numbers are increasing year on year.

PART 3

Future Trends—Sectors and Destinations

Travel Sectors

Trends in the way travelers research and make decisions about their final choice of destination are emerging from the various sources of data we have covered so far. The places they search for inspiration, and the way they access different media, are rapidly changing across all demographic groups but particularly for the growing mature sector. It can also be seen that what they are looking for and expect from providers in the tourism and travel industry has become broader, more specific, and in many cases outside the traditional view of what an older traveler wants.

We can see from the examples of country profiles discussed earlier what patterns of travel have been up until now, particularly the increasing numbers of those in the 55+ and more mature 65+ age groups that want to expand their experience of the world. In many cases, there is a link with the sector or type of traveler we have touched on briefly earlier. It is useful to think about these elements in more detail, what it is that makes them an important factor in the decision-making process, before we discuss growing trends in finding new destinations to visit.

Luxury Travel

The luxury travel sector is expanding rapidly, many commentators seeing this as a clear link with the target group who are considered to be the ones with the most disposable income available. If no longer in full-time employment, or with no immediate family or small children to consider in their final choice of experience to book, they may indeed be ideally placed to enjoy a luxury break. This is a significant trend going forward into 2020. The large-scale Condé Nast 2019 survey, for instance, highlighted opportunities for luxury travel to many locations seen as upcoming destinations for both U.S. and UK markets.

Rural estates continue to be popular destinations and are predicted (Condé Nast 2019) to continue as attractive holiday options at the luxury end. Newer offerings that intend to widen the experience for the guest, such as a working farm in South Africa or a vineyard in rural France, sit alongside traditional country estates such as Gleneagles in Scotland, UK. For such experiences, marketing efforts and publicity materials incorporate reference to the luxury facilities available.

Often this is extended to include reference to the use of freshly grown and picked local produce, expertly prepared on site by a star-quality chef, thus reducing its environmental impact. Even cows in 2000 acres of pasture belonging to an 11th century castle in France, Domaine des Etangs, are mentioned as an attractive feature of this luxury retreat, a reference to the idyllic rural life in the distant past (Condé Nast 2019).

Self-Catering Accommodation

Traditionally considered to be at the opposite end to luxury travel, certainly in the UK, there has been a significant increase in numbers choosing this option. An interesting example of taking the basic premise of renting self-catering accommodation to a higher level, in various price ranges, is the growing Airbnb concept. While other evidence suggests only a small percent of customers would choose to book through Airbnb and hotels are still the most popular choice for the majority of mature travelers, Airbnb found the 50+ and intergeneration groups are particularly keen to consider what is on offer through this option to book.

City breaks are consistently a popular option for accommodation-only bookings and renting a holiday villa with all the facilities and home comforts at hand has long been a feature of travel for UK families. It is interesting to see how this room-only option has also been extended to include opulent, palatial accommodation such as Jaipur's City Palace in India, the first of its kind to be listed on Airbnb.

Though such properties may not offer the same features needed to attract the eco-friendly conscious client, there is clearly a market for those seeking an exciting new experience (Travel Weekly 2019) such as staying at rooms in the Palace of Versailles, Holyrood Palace, or even a Tuscan estate sleeping 14 people at Castello Uglione in Italy (Condé Nast 2019).

Solo Travel

We have briefly mentioned implications for the solo traveler earlier, the critical point being that this refers to "solo" travel, not "single travelers."

Silver Travel Advisor carried out a separate survey on solo travel with 500 respondents and identified some interesting issues. While 55 percent of respondents said they had no one else to travel with, 41 percent stated they have a partner at home, a finding echoed in the recent Mintel survey that showed 32 percent of their solo traveler respondents had a partner and so were not "single." If you look more closely at the responses, 30 percent (Silver Travel Advisor 2020) noted that they have very different interests from their partner, while 20 percent just preferred to travel alone. This response was also a feature of the Titan Travel survey.

A regular comment from their more mature customers is how the opportunity to visit places their partner is unwilling, or unable, to travel to is an attractive option. For Titan Travel customers in particular, the advantage of their service is that it starts straightaway with pickup from the home address to the first travel point (airport, rail station, or port) with a designated driver. The most significant trend for them in 2020 has been a substantial rise in bookings from solo travelers for river cruises offering considerably lower single supplements than other providers for similar trips.

The surge in baby boomers booking solo trips is also seen in research from Solo Traveler World. They found that around 40 percent of travelers worldwide took a solo trip in 2017–2018, and a further 21 percent planned to do so in the future (Solo Traveler World 2019).

Top solo destinations in 2019 were Turkey, Egypt, Greece, Australia, the Scottish Highlands, France, Central America, and New Orleans. Escorted tours that include these destinations have a growing market within the mature solo travel cohort.

Accessible Travel for Those with Disabilities

There are many examples and case studies that suggest the UK is leading the way to ensure everyone can access appropriate provision as this continues to be a growing trend.

The following examples are a clear indication of where accessibility can be a positive incentive for prospective clients, particularly as they are generally accompanied by family members or carers who make up the party booking.

- Virgin Holidays has an assistance line for customers and agents to ensure bookings can meet any special needs.
- Encompass offers a disability travel consultancy service providing advice and guidance for travel companies.
- Traveleyes arranges breaks for blind or partially sighted clients accompanied by their "seeing" companion.
- Enable Holidays provides guidance on access and adapted vehicle transfers within the destination country.
- Limitless Travel provides social care personnel on fully accessible UK coach tours to ensure the safety and welfare of guests traveling with them.
- Revitalise Respite Holidays has nurse-led care at three resorts in the UK, allowing some respite breaks with full-time care responsibilities.
- Forest Holidays has hoists fitted in specially adapted woodland cabins so that everyone can enjoy the hot tubs!
- Driving Miss Daisy offers adapted vehicle transfers from home to airports, cruise terminals, rail and coach stations within the UK.
- Dementia Adventure offers a range of UK breaks for dementia sufferers and those who care for them, making sure that guests can enjoy exciting experiences not otherwise available to them.
- Personal Touch Holidays now offers dementia-friendly trips to Portugal.

There are many more examples internationally that provide accommodation and activities that can be enjoyed by everyone in the group, and certainly there are many new products coming onto the market that can assist an individual with limited mobility.

Multigeneration Travel

Multigeneration travel is also a significant trend for 2020 in the escorted tour sector, not just booking a family size villa or beach break (Titan Travel 2019–2020). There are lots of reasons for this rising trend, not just as a baby-sitting service. Parents with grown-up children may wish to celebrate a special occasion, a reward for achievement, a special birthday or anniversary, or just a chance to relax and get closer as a family unit.

As noted previously, some cruise liners are being opened up specifically as a multigeneration package, and currently 56 percent of U.S. travel agents offer multigeneration packages. Travelzoo's survey of 1,700 respondents (Travelzoo 2019) found 83 percent said the main reason they chose a multigeneration package was to spend quality time together. In addition, 28 percent said the chance to explore new places together as an extended family was important and 26 percent cited the chance to eat and socialize together was a crucial reason behind their decision to book.

Virgin Holidays surveyed 1,000 parents and 1,000 grandparents who had taken a holiday together to see how each different age/family stage group viewed the multigeneration option. While 25 percent of grandparents said they enjoyed it more than when they holidayed by themselves, it was no surprise that 1/3 of parents liked the access to extra help looking after the children. When asked what they would do differently next time, the main changes would be to go abroad rather than stay in the home country, have more flexible mealtimes, and choose an all-inclusive package to cover all the incidental food and refreshment costs inevitable with accompanying children. Interestingly, a large proportion said the next time they would stay nearby but not on the same resort to give everyone the space to choose what they wanted to do. Both groups identified that it was also important to discuss the choice of activities at the planning stage rather than work it out once on vacation.

Escorted tours where all the travel and accommodation details are arranged are clearly being seen as a valuable option, and as Titan Travel states, their offering of "escorted" tours is much more flexible than earlier options and has many more opportunities for tailor-made provision.

Destinations—Where Do They Want to Go in the Future?

From a UK perspective, the target group is generally taking more holidays and spending more money while away than they did in previous years. In 2018 there were 71.7 million trips overseas, up 29 percent on 2012–2017 statistics (ONS 2018–2019). Interestingly, the average length of each trip decreased from 10.4 nights to 9.8 nights, but the total money spent increased by 1 percent to £45.4 billion, around £633 per person per trip.

However, note that future trends for destinations are often linked to exchange rates between currencies; whether this is the $US, £GBP, or Euro, this appears as an issue when customers are making the final decision of where to go (US Travel Association 2019).

The Oddfellows Travel group survey found 64 percent named the top choice of destination within the UK as England, rather than other parts of Britain such as Wales, Scotland, or Northern Ireland, and Europe as the main destination outside of the UK for 85 percent of respondents. Note that this is a fairly small survey sample rather than a large research study, so results are not necessarily true of the overall picture for the UK mature travel market. They do, however, broadly reflect findings from other surveys.

The Titan Travel survey identified that the top five choices of destination for British travelers have changed little in recent years, with the United States, Canada, Italy, India, and South Africa remaining the primary attractions. Crucially, there are many deterrents identified by potential visitors to the United States from all nationalities, which do need to be addressed. Many of them may indeed be perceptions rather than reality, so much of the action must be to overcome the negative concerns in the promotion and marketing materials.

Other regions are moving up the list, particularly Peru and Costa Rica, Vietnam, China, and Japan. As we have seen earlier, the rapidly rising choices are Uzbekistan and Borneo, both recently featured in national TV programs, so clearly this form of promotion has been successful with the target group.

Riviera Travel found 72 percent of customers mentioned that the best time to enjoy travel is over the age of 55, a clear target group of mature travelers. Table 38 illustrates what their customers wanted as their "wish list" of destinations for future travel, with no real surprises compared with previous surveys (Riviera Travel 2020). Following feedback from customers, they have continued to add new destinations and travel experiences for 2020–2021.

Table 38 Wish list of destinations for the future (UK)

Order of preference	Place to visit
1	Niagara Falls
2	Petra
3	Machu Picchu
4	Yosemite National Park
5	Great Wall of China
6	Blue Lagoon Iceland
7	Taj Mahal
8	Pompeii
9	Galapagos Islands
10	Acropolis Athens

Image 8 Niagara Falls [Photo by J Jeynes]

Readers of the *Daily Mail* and the *Mail on Sunday* were asked where they were hoping to travel to in the next five years (to 2024), and although there are some differences in the reader profiles compared with Riviera Travel, their choices were very similar (Table 39).

Table 39 Future destinations in descending order of preference (UK)

Daily Mail (%)		Mail on Sunday (%)	
44	Canada or United States	46	Europe mainland
39	Europe mainland	43	Canada or United States
34	UK	34	UK
32	Australia	31	Australia
30	South America	31	South America
28	Asia	28	Asia
25	Middle East	25	Middle East
23	Africa	23	Africa

Canada continues to be an attractive destination for UK travelers, particularly the experience of riding "Rocky Mountaineer" train between Banff and Vancouver over two days. As well as British tourists, its key markets are Canada and the United States, Australia, and New Zealand, with a customer base generally in the 55+ age group.

Though not a sleeper train, its focus is on offering a premium train experience, luxury travel with purpose-built viewing lounges, first class food, and unrivaled levels of service. Rocky Mountaineer celebrates 30 years in 2020, having "welcomed more than two million guests" since 1990 and doubled its capacity since 2014. The focus continues to be on the three core routes between Vancouver and the Canadian Rockies with a new service offered in Mandarin for travelers from China (Rocky Mountaineer 2020).

Existing popular experiences of rail travel across Australia, Africa, the Canadian Rockies, Europe, plus new additions linking existing long-distance rail journeys such as in Australia, are an indication of the growing potential within the mature market. A particularly good option currently being promoted through sites such as www.trainline.com is the Euro-wide ticket that allows you to plan your trip yet still giving the flexibility for hop on–hop off to explore and sightsee if you fancy. This service

Image 9 Rocky Mountaineer train [Photo by Rocky Mountaineer]

has expanded and clearly attracts those who want to experience a feeling of adventure but within a structured self-planned program (The Trainline .com 2019).

We have seen that the U.S. traveler intends to visit Europe more often than previously, although Table 40 shows European destinations were also the most popular in 2017. Tour operators and travel agents are seeing a shift in preferred destinations since 2017, Table 40 offering some useful insights into what has changed (USTOA) though not the reasons why.

Table 40 Future destinations in descending order of preference (United States)

2017	2019	Emerging 2020–2025
Mexico	Italy	Iceland
Italy	Iceland	Cambodia
Germany	Japan	Croatia
France	Vietnam	Colombia
UK	Australia	Vietnam
Netherlands	France	Portugal
Spain	Spain	Bhutan
Ireland	Colombia	Bolivia
Switzerland	Cambodia	Myanmar
Australia	Portugal	Ethiopia

More waterways are opening up for cruise craft with the opportunity for attractions along the route to increase their profile. Food and wine consistently appear near the top of the list for what people are looking for, so river (and rail) travel provides an ideal opportunity to give added value to an existing trip.

Profile of Travel Destinations and Attractions in the UK

The UK—England, Wales, Scotland, Northern Ireland

The UK continues to be a popular destination for tourists globally and Visit England, set up to promote tourism in England (rather than the UK as a whole), found a significant increase in overnight stays during the first six months of 2019, rising to 35 million nights spent. Major cities outside London are popular with both overseas tourists and domestic visitors, with the focus on history and architectural features, restaurants, and the arts.

A growing trend is for visitors to tour scenic routes and more remote places such as coastal paths and small islands around the British coastline. The Ramblers Association is a long-standing organization that provides information about many routes for either short- or long-distance walking. They have established Ramblers Cruise and Walk Holidays, in conjunction with Adagio cultural tours, to combine activities in one package aimed primarily at mature travelers in several countries (Ramblers Holidays 2020).

Long-distance paths, such as those along the borders between Wales and England in the west or Scotland and England in the north, are regularly walked by couples or small groups, again a large proportion of them in the 55+ age group. In some areas, service providers have emerged offering to transport luggage between overnight accommodation, saving walkers the need to carry all of their kit with them for the whole journey.

In the UK, the sleeper train between London and Scotland has been relaunched (the Caledonian Sleeper), and new travel experiences in Scotland are appearing. For example, a bespoke tour company is offering unique opportunities to enjoy traditional outdoor pursuits on the estate of a Scottish Lord or a stay in one of nine apartments in Holyrood Palace from 2020. Clearly there are opportunities for such rail experiences to be a significant part of packages offered as the content is such a crucial element of the final decision to book.

Large country house hotels continue to be popular, especially as a luxury break, but are becoming more family-friendly, with options to stay outside the main house rather than in the main body of the hotel. For example, the country hotel Lucknam Park offers a stay in the Squire's Cottage or Keeper's Cottage, either option remaining part of the hotel service. They include outdoor activities as well as spa facilities, so are ideal for multigeneration groups. Luxury short breaks, such as lodges with hot tubs, were searched for online by 20 percent of visitors to England.

Image 10 Spectacular British Castle [Photo by Red Zeppelin]

While this trend continues to grow in the UK, it is clear that such properties cannot rely only on being a beautiful house and grounds without something extra to entice potential customers. The main reasons cited by the UK market for choosing a vacation in their home country were the perceived higher levels of safety and security, concern post-Brexit about medical care costs and travel insurance when going abroad, and the increasing pet-friendly options available. As with the trends generally in the travel market, choosing a domestic destination is seen as a greener option especially if traveling by train.

Canals were the lifeblood of the industrial landscape in Britain between the mid-19th and early 20th centuries, in the same way that a variety of waterways have been in many countries, but their decline in the context of transporting goods has opened up many new leisure and tourist opportunities throughout the UK. The towpath running along-side hundreds of miles of canal systems is perfect for walking or cycling, mainly level ground, so perfect for the growing numbers of mature walkers. A more recent trend is for these paths to be developed further, providing several sections that are accessible for those with some mobility restrictions. In some areas, public transport runs fairly close to the canal, in some cases with a Bike Trailer fitted to the back of the bus during summer months, so that walkers or cyclists can cover a reasonable distance and get back to their starting point without just retracing their steps.

River and canal craft have also featured widely in the UK TV programs aimed at the mature viewer. Retired, veteran personalities demonstrate how easily (or not!) it is to navigate canal locks, suggesting an impressively calm and easy-going form of travel through rural and urban landscapes.

Image 11 Boats on the canal [Photo by James Homans]

Although we have seen research that suggests the mature sector is not particularly impressed by celebrity endorsements of a product or service, there is clear evidence that bookings for trips to the destinations featured in such films increase immediately following a TV broadcast (Titan Travel 2019–2020).

We know that the mature sector is keen to find new places to explore and is always interested in learning about new food products, especially when it involves tastings and sampling where these products are actually produced. Certainly, the food and drink sectors are increasingly featured in TV series, both in Britain and overseas, with an ever-increasing number of celebrity chefs exploring products and ways to produce new dishes based on home-grown specialty foods.

For this target group, wine (and food) is regularly mentioned as a feature they are looking for, so tours of vineyards, wine tastings, and more structured "courses" have significant potential to add to tourist numbers. Though not necessarily considered a wine-making region, there has been a rapid increase in the number of vineyards and distilleries in many parts of Britain, with many wines taking prestigious prizes in international competitions. Special interest short cruises, themed cruises, and river cruises around the UK, including Christmas Market shopping trips, have seen an increase as we go into 2020 (Titan Travel 2019–2020).

Image 12 Wine tasting at Kerry Vale Vineyard [Photo by J Jeynes]

Profile of Potential International Travel Destinations and Attractions

This section includes a brief summary of features related to destinations identified as potential go-to places in the future. It is not a comprehensive list, of course, as there are so many new destinations being developed and aimed at the more mature traveler. But it is intended to give a snapshot of some areas that have the potential to provide more options, to engage the traveler in the added adventure and experience of new places that this market group has already identified they want.

Most of these destinations are featured in "wish lists," country profiles, and large-scale survey responses for the Condé Nast report in 2019 (Condé Nast 2019).

Image 13 Cruise ship [Photo by Anthony Metcalfe]

A significant change in the last two decades has been the option to fly to the start destination for an ocean cruise, thus reducing the sail time on ocean crossings and therefore cost to the customer. This fits closely with changes in what the 50+ market is looking for (see earlier notes), a more immediate result, rather than for the older target group that may still have the time and funds to enjoy a longer cruise.

The recent increased interest in the river cruise market, more appealing to many than ocean cruises, is in part due to the opportunity to see a country from a different perspective, whether in your home country or traveling overseas. A major attraction is the luxury of all-inclusive accommodation and travel at a much slower pace.

India/Asia

One of the main features associated with India (for those who have not visited) is the beautiful Taj Mahal in Agra, the marble mausoleum built by

Shah Jahan in memory of his beloved wife Mumtaz, yet the continent has so much more to offer. From a UK perspective, there have recently been celebrity road trips shown on TV and films that feature opportunities for older retired people to live in India. "Bollywood" is growing in popularity around the world, so there is already a close affinity with the continent for many potential visitors.

When we consider locations worldwide that are struggling with overcapacity tourism, including the Taj Mahal and the Golden Triangle, there is an opportunity for tour operators to expand their provision and focus on other elements of the culture. For India, these are likely to include the colorful foods and spices, rich silk fabrics, and elaborate architecture.

Example

Explore! This tour operator offers a trip across the middle of India rather than the Golden Triangle, traveling through Hyderabad across country and by local train for the final stage to Goa. It is a stunning journey with the opportunity to visit majestic temples and ornate palaces as well as a chance to see the real India without contributing to overtourism.

Image 14 Indian temple [Photo by J Jeynes]

Egypt

Since 2011, Egypt has been a difficult location to promote as local unrest and personal security has been a major issue, both for visitors and for those who have planned expansion of services and accommodation. By 2018, it had fewer visitors in a year than the British Museum in London (A. Sattin, Condé Nast). Currently (2020), the situation has improved considerably, and promotion of visitor options has increased, particularly through travel agencies.

Image 15 Pyramid at Giza [Photo by Simon Matzinger]

Apart from the traditional attractions associated with Egypt that tourists may have seen on previous visits, such as the pyramids at Giza, there are other features to explore.

Visitors and travel agents might consider including a trip to central Cairo and the new museum, which is now the final space for the world-renowned Tutankhamun exhibition. Other potential excursions include sailing on a traditional felucca boat to Aswan or exploring the exotic and unusual plants on show in the botanical gardens.

For the mature traveler, background research into the destination is common, so provision of, or links to, sources of historical information is seen as a positive extra. Although current views on the dress code for tourists is changing, the issue of personal safety and security remains a potential block when customers are considering Egypt as one of the final two to three options to book.

Northern Sudan

As a potential new market, Northern Sudan is becoming more accessible to visitors, with positive steps being taken to promote what it has to offer. As in Egypt, it has its own array of pyramids, ancient cities with an additional option to "camp" in the dunes of Nubian Desert and stargaze beneath clear night skies with no light pollution. It is a new and exciting destination that few will have been to as a tourist. It has the potential to offer the chance to explore new territories, which is an increasingly attractive option for mature travelers and therefore increase visitor numbers.

Saudi Arabia

At the time of writing, Saudi Arabia is a fantastic new opportunity for travelers looking for something new as it has only recently (September 2019) made visitor visas available. Most potential customers have little knowledge of what there is to see if you visit, so there is a lot of work needed by tour operators to raise awareness and encourage them to include it as a potential destination.

Image 16 Saudi Arabia mosque [Photo by Adli Wahid]

It is a wealthy nation with much to offer the visitor, whether super-scale architectural features or the luxury of 5-star accommodation.

Several renewable energy projects are underway, including installing a tropical reef archipelago, and they are opening up impressive ancient landmarks, such as Jeddah, to tourists from overseas as well as domestic Saudi nationals.

Unrest in the Middle East continues to be a potential problem for tourism generally; so, in reality, such opportunities that exist may be limited at the beginning of 2020. As we have seen already, personal safety and security is an issue for many when they are making their final decisions before completing a booking, so some sort of assurances need to be identified beforehand.

Image 17 Saudi desert [Photo by Sebastien]

Kuwait and Dubai

Staying within the Middle East region, Kuwait and Dubai are identified as a future trend in destinations for overseas visitors.

Kuwait is known for its varied cuisine, appealing to the mature traveler looking for new culinary experiences. Dubai is rapidly expanding its reputation from being a high-powered business center to one of adventure in its expansive sand dunes and mountains.

Visits to museums and sites of historical interest are consistently high on the list of content a planned package must include, so this region has a great deal to offer the tourist. The recently opened National Museum of Qatar, Dubai's Museum of the Future, and the Petra Museum include exceptional exhibition spaces that allow the visitor to see and experience its cultural heritage. The museum hub of Abu Dhabi's Saadiyat Island is a

Image 18 Splendid Dubai [Photo by Nick Fewings]

unique experience within an unusual and visually stunning setting. This would certainly be a positive option for anyone interested in learning about the arts and the cultural heritage of a new destination.

Japan

As we have seen in survey responses and country profiles discussed earlier, there has been a rapid increase in the popularity of Japan as a tourist destination in recent years. Many things have contributed to this, including international events such as the international Rugby World Cup games in 2019 and a continuing fascination with the culture and traditions of Japan, whether real or imagined! For instance, there is a long tradition of visits by both domestic and overseas tourists to witness the stunning show

Image 19 Geishas [Photo by Sorasak]

of cherry blossom around March time. Fashion Month Fukuoka Kyushu (www.f-month.com) in March is also a growing visitor attraction.

Note there has been a backlash related to tourists stopping Geishas in Kyoto for photograph opportunities, and again there are several hotspots that are suffering overtourism including Mount Fuji and the capital city Tokyo.

Environmental issues have become more prevalent in the last few years with concerns about safety and natural disasters. Earthquakes and volcano activity in the wider region, including Japan and New Zealand, are a sobering reminder of the need to balance tourist activity and income with environmental factors and safety.

Australia

The scale and size of Australia and what it has to offer is often underestimated. It is interesting to see how the long-distance rail journeys have been expanded so that people can see more of the "real" Australia (see previous notes on rail travel). The beginning of 2020 has seen one of the biggest wildfire disasters in Australia covering huge areas of land mass and threatening lives, wildlife, and homes. This was actually confined to one region in the west of Australia, rather than over the whole land mass, but it will be interesting to see how rapidly they can recover and engage with tourists that contribute so much to their economy.

Image 20 Sydney Opera House [Photo by Srikant Sahoo]

Given its size, Australia has long had transcontinental trains running from Darwin to Adelaide (the Ghan) and from Perth to Sydney (the Indian Pacific). The year 2020 has seen the addition of another long-distance sleeper train offering a three-day trip on the Great Southern from Adelaide and Brisbane. Australian tour operator "Journey Beyond" is promoting this trip as the ideal of old-style luxury and adventure that we have seen appeals to the mature traveler. This does, therefore, recognize and reflect the trend in extending slower forms of travel and meets the changing needs of our target group.

Image 21 Australia train [Photo by Hamish Weir]

Cambodia

Cambodia has specifically been identified by U.S. travel organizations as an up-and-coming destination. Many new initiatives being developed for tourists include the two islands of Song Saa with their overwater purpose-built villas, upcycled furnishings, and the owners' foundation, which has been established to support the surrounding natural environment. This is a good example of combining a range of elements that are important to the target sector and so a worthwhile destination to explore further.

Africa

Image 22 Namibia sky [Photo by Harry Cunningham]

Often associated with safari expeditions, which are growing in popularity as visitors are seeking more than just the scenery, there is clearly much more to Africa that will attract new visitors. If research shows that the target group of travelers are primarily interested in culture, history, food, and wine, Africa has immense potential for more targeted promotion that incorporates these elements as part of the overall package.

Rwanda is not a country most mature travelers consider as a holiday destination given its history of conflict. However, it is starting to develop options that include visiting the Virunga Mountains and the Volcanoes National Park. As with other regions of Africa, it is potentially a new market to explore further.

Zimbabwe still has economic problems (in 2020) but is considered safe to visit (Condé Nast 2019) if using a specialist local tour guide rather than arranging a package alone. It has the potential to appeal to the target group as an adventure trip, as long as safety is the clear message for providers to consider when developing it as a new destination.

Tanzania, already known as a safari destination, is attracting major hotel chains that offer luxury accommodation and organize trips that encompass all the magical sights of the national parks in full 5-star style. The additional message emerging from here is sustainability and the environmentally friendly use of natural resources to reduce the tourist impact.

Image 23 Precious forest Africa [Photo by Hans Eiskonen]

South Africa has long been an attractive destination for tourists with its majestic scenery, varied plant species, and as a wine-making region, although this is not necessarily the case for other parts of the continent. There is so much more to Africa that can appeal to the mature sector, whatever their age group or interests, so more needs to be done to pro-mote what is on offer to a wider market that has already suggested they would be interested.

South America

There is clearly potential to expand tourism within South America as a target destination for many mature travelers in the future (USTOA 2018). Peru continues to be an attractive destination, with Machu Picchu a hiker's challenge and one often taken up by mature travelers to raise funds for charity. Note that this is another destination identified as suffering from damage associated with overtourism. Venezuela has suffered from political uncertainty for a while so is not viewed as a positive destination at present. This too had been a favorite hiking destination in the past, from Merida to the Andes, with one of the highest cable cars, an ice cream shop selling hundreds of different flavors, and an opportunity to see the cumbersome Condor laboriously plodding up the hillside to reach a high enough point to launch itself in flight (it cannot take off from flat ground level!).

Cultural visits to Patagonia are particularly popular for those from Wales in the UK, as their Welsh descendants made the hazardous journey to this southern part of South America in the 19th century and the Welsh language is still spoken there.

Image 24 Stunning lake in South America [Photo by Arto Marttinen]

Some areas of South America are still considered unsafe for visitors, and a recent attack on a wealthy visitor identified as a target on arrival at the airport does not help. As before, personal safety and security is a critical issue for all travel agencies and tour operators to consider.

Alaska

Alaska is certainly growing as a potential destination for travelers, identified by U.S. and other survey respondents further afield. It is still perceived as an "epic" landscape with extremes of weather and a timeless feel that brings out the pioneer/adventurer in visitors (apparently!) (H Pearson, Condé Nast). It has regularly been featured as an add-on trip for those visiting Canada and the United States but has developed its individual character as a new exciting destination in its own right so it continues to be part of future travel trends.

Image 25 Alaskan train [Photo by Anna Tremewan]

PART 4

Strategies

You cannot lump them all together as one target consumer

If research shows that mature travelers, whether 50+, 60+, or 70+, do not recognize themselves in advertisements, this must be a starting point for providers to consider. An interesting point made by Debbie Marshall, director of Silver Travel Advisor, is that most marketing campaigns aimed at 50+ are produced by those in their 30s. Feedback from many sources highlights the widening range of activities that mature travelers across all age groups are seeking. There may indeed be continuing demand for trips associated with mature sectors, such as ocean cruising and city breaks, but this target sector is much more IT savvy than was the case even five years ago. They want to be inspired and are looking for something new.

Given the significance of travel and tourism to all countries worldwide, there has to be some form of strategic plan to make the most of all the existing and emerging opportunities for reaching and retaining potential travelers. While 2020 presents huge challenges for tourism globally, the situation with COVID-19 will eventually change.

Taking one country as an example, the strategic decision by Mexico to close 17 of its 21 Tourism Board offices around the world is an interesting discussion point. Whatever the result of this for Mexico in the future, it does open up a real opportunity for tour operators, travel agents, and a wide range of private travel marketing companies to take up where the Mexican tourist board left off. We have already seen how Mexico is a growing market, gradually moving up the various lists of places visited or being explored as a possible destination, so it is a significant course of action to monitor over the next few years.

While it raises many questions for the outside observer, there was an important reason behind this decision. Mexico's stated motive (US Travel Association 2019) is to use the substantial $300 million saved in order to develop a rail link along the Mayan Peninsula, which is intended to promote tourism and economic growth in more rural and less developed areas of the Yucatán Peninsula. Given our discussions earlier about the need to find more travel destinations that will ease the pressure on the popular bucket list destinations around the world, and indeed to promote rail travel rather than air, this could well be a positive strategy for the mature travel sector.

For the United States, there are several issues related to losing market share that need a strategic approach in the coming years in order to raise their competitive edge. The decline in numbers of inbound tourists from Germany, Japan, China, and Canada needs to be addressed sooner rather than later. Even if there is no decline in numbers at present, competition is growing from newer tourist attractions and those that take a positive approach to the trends identified.

There is so much data available on motivations of travelers to the United States, where they want to visit when they get there, and the overall content of their trip, which can inform new approaches to making the United States an attractive destination again. The same is true for all nations where tourism is a large part of their economic growth.

Data Collection and Collation

We have seen some detailed large-scale survey results already, from information and review sites, providers of products or services, and organizations that collect and disseminate data within the tourism industry. While providers will have their own sources of data, including input from their existing client base, there are clearly many more routes to gaining relevant data to support strategic decision-making.

The latest survey from DMA, Consumer Email Tracker 2020, provides some insights into habits of older users compared with those of younger age groups (DMA 2020). For instance, they found that e-mail is still the best way to attract and engage with customers in the 45+ to 65+ age groups.

The majority check their inbox at least once a day, 62 percent of those in the 55 to 64 age group confirm they do so, and 74 percent of the 65+ age group state they check daily. The majority use Gmail as their personal address and also prefer to use their PC rather than a mobile device to read their e-mail messages (Table 41).

Table 41 Preference to view e-mails on PC

Age group (years)	% who prefer to use PC
45–54	48
55–64	61
65+	73

The recent introduction of General Data Protection Regulation (GDPR) that states how personal information can be stored or used by providers of products or services, and the requirement for individuals to opt in or out of use of their data by brands, has not made this age group feel more confident. Less than half of survey respondents aged 55+ felt more confident about how their data is used now GDPR is in place, but more than a third said they were still unsure about how a brand had gained knowledge of their personal e-mail address.

DMA suggests that brand marketers need to make it clearer, and perhaps more explicit, what the opt in/opt out requirement actually means in practice. It would help to ensure any marketing e-mails received were seen as personal to them rather than just random advertising. The full report makes interesting reading with more detail about the effective use of e-mail marketing. It can be accessed via their website (DMA 2020).

EyeforTravel is one of many websites that discusses collecting and collating data to get a clearer picture of what potential customers actually want. In particular, it includes insights into how you can track users across all their devices they might use to research sites and even to track usage across different parts of your own business where there may be multiple or portfolio options that cover relevant material to their search. They stress the importance of personalizing messages and looking at geographic differences in booking patterns whether related to time of year, advance planning for specific events (such as the Rugby World Cup in

Japan 2019—see later discussion), school or work shutdowns (Eyefor-Travel 2020).

ADARA is an example of a number of firms that provide Predictive Traveler Intelligence, in this case based on data provided by over 200 travel industry partners. Their approach is explained in detail in their recent publication "Travel Marketing Strategies: 18 Strategies for Conquering 5 Key Travel Marketing Goals." While the intention is not to reproduce the whole report here—it can be found via their website of course—there are some critical elements that support the development of strategies based on our findings discussed so far (ADARA 2019).

Their approach is intended to help those responsible for marketing their travel services by using relevant data to understand patterns, trends, and behaviors of customers. We have already identified some patterns and trends within the target sector of mature travelers, but these are generalized across geographic borders and different data sources. The ADARA report provides a valuable starting point for anyone involved in developing marketing strategies for their travel organization.

ADARA's definitions and categories of buyers are a useful starting point for deciding where these fit within a strategic marketing plan. Their categories are based on travel intentions, buyer characteristics, a profile of what they have booked before, and a closer breakdown of their shopping profile to help classify group tendencies. The information is assumed to be available through your existing online statistics, although, as with any research to identify trends, it may involve interpretation and evaluation of the data.

Travel intentions can be based on visitors to your site, such as:

- someone who has recently searched for or booked a trip with you,
- those who have already booked and are due to depart within the next one to three months, and
- those who are already at their destination and recently booked an extra trip or activity while there.

Buyer characteristics are drawn from data for:

- Travelers who were looking for luxury, top-end breaks where content is more important than the price

- Bargain hunters who want a good deal, a value for money break—it may be that they want to take more trips during the year so want to spread the available funds further
- The last-minute traveler, sometimes booking business trips, where price is not the primary concern

Profile based on the type of trip they have booked before, such as:

- Leisure travel breaks
- Business trips to a range of destinations
- Whether they previously chose International or domestic breaks/vacations
- Whether they booked luxury trips at the top end of price range or went for budget packages
- If they traveled as a family group, as a solo traveler, or as a couple
- Choosing and booking last-minute trips purely for leisure

Further segmentation can help to identify "look-alikes"—those who fit the profile of others to narrow down individual options and identify target groups:

- multibrand shoppers who use a range of different channels to research and book a trip
- those who have shown they are willing to buy an upgrade as part of their package, when they book, if offered the option to do so
- those who choose a package at the luxury end and are prepared to upgrade part of the booking at a later stage
- customers who wait until they have arrived at the destination before considering making an additional booking
- shoppers who are loyal to a brand—they have an affinity with a certain brand and tend to be loyal to it when making their purchasing decision

As you can see, such market data (specific to your customer base) provides a detailed picture that will help define ways to reach the key travel goals you have identified. In particular, the data helps to focus on the segments that are likely to produce the greatest return on your marketing activity.

From ADARA's research, they have identified the following "Five Key Travel Marketing Goals":

- Brand awareness
- Customer engagement
- Acquiring new customers
- Direct booking conversions
- Ancillary revenue

It does not matter which order you place these goals in as they are obviously linked to each other and are just as relevant if placed as a continuous circle. What they do require is detailed analysis of existing customers and traffic to your website and social media platforms, which is not such an easy task in reality.

As we have seen in earlier discussions, it is not enough to rely on consistent loyalty from customers. If the "Think with Google" survey results show anything valuable in this context, it is that fewer than 10 percent of U.S. travelers know which brand they will ultimately book with until they have done some wider research. Even with Elite Loyalty Program membership, more than two-thirds would pick a different hotel if it is available at a better price, and two-thirds of members of air loyalty programs would choose a different airline if the route, timing, and price were better.

The segmentation elements listed above demonstrate that brand promotion may need to be more focused and targeted toward selected groupings. This is important for existing customers as well as potential new ones, and as mentioned previously our mature target sector is extremely varied in profile. As with all marketing activity, one approach will not necessarily fit everyone you are trying to reach.

Customer engagement is an interesting point that needs further analysis. Current research results have shown more contradictions here than on any other subject. The ADARA report (from 200 travel industry partners) says 87 percent of customers wanted more personalization in communications and campaigns but only 64 percent said they got it. This report does not differentiate between age groups and so may not reflect the position for the mature sector.

The Buying Habits survey (ATTEST 2019) noted that 79 percent of millennials found personalization acceptable but 44 percent of baby boomers did not. For it to be a successful part of the strategy, the background data has to be reliable and of sufficient depth to really help distinguish the customer profile.

Attracting new customers is always a key goal, particularly as brand loyalty is not an absolute long-term concept, as is converting those who have shown an interest but not completed a booking. Again, the ADARA approach is a useful one, thinking about repeat buyers, "look-alikes" with similar buying patterns, and reaching out to prospective new customers (Table 42).

Table 42 Key goals, target groups, and ways to reach them

Key goal	Target group	Ways to reach them
Increase booking conversions	In-market, who have recently searched or booked online	Website/e-mail/app/social media/direct mail
Fill unsold inventory	Previous last-minute leisure Bookers/in-market group	E-mail/app
Increase off-season bookings	Peak season non-bookers with off-season offers	Social media
Increase bookings	Direct bookers—leisure and business	Website/e-mail/app/social media
Attract new customers	In-market/according to value score system—non-bookers	Website/email/social media
Retarget those who abandoned the booking path	Direct bookers/according to value score system that shows high likelihood of booking	Website/e-mail/social media/direct mail

While this reflects standard marketing practice, it is vital to stress the importance of appropriate, detailed data collection in order to produce a clearer picture of different segments within the potential customer base.

ADARA produces a wide range of statistical reports and more detailed case studies that illustrate the practical application of their research findings. One that is relevant to this discussion is the following case study of travel insights into the Rugby World Cup in Japan in 2019.

Case Study: ADARA Report—Rugby World Cup Fan Travel Insights 2019

This is a fascinating look at travel planning and booking actions related to a specific global event—the Rugby World Cup held in Japan from September 20 to November 2, 2019. It focuses on inbound flight bookings that include a minimum stay of five days during the event or at least two days afterward. The main nations they (ADARA) identified as popular rugby supporters for this study were:

- Australia and New Zealand
- UK, Ireland, Italy, France
- Canada
- Argentina, Uruguay
- South Africa

Over the period of the event, travelers from these countries made up between 5 and 20 percent of inbound visitors, rising to over 30 percent once play started on September 20 and approximately 40 percent just before the November 2 final. It is fascinating to see in Table 43 the percentage rise in visitor numbers to Japan (compared with the year before) related to country of origin, especially from Ireland!

Table 43 Percentage rise in visitors to Japan for Rugby World Cup based on country of origin

	September 2019% rise	October 2019% rise
Australia	32.2	48.4
UK	37.2	63.5
Canada	41.9	55.7
Ireland	293.3	394.3

Around 40 percent of visitors booked between October 2018 and August 2019, early but not cheaper and actually spent more on airfare than those who booked nearer the time. However, 22 percent of these did stay for longer—for at least 21 days. Nearly half of visitors during this event, 47.8 percent, did not book until September 2019, just before the start of play, and 17.8 percent stayed for more than 21 days.

Those from Europe were more likely to visit as couples, but for those from Australia and New Zealand it was more likely to be as groups of three or more; 40 percent of those from Europe booked business or first class air travel and therefore spent much more on their air fare at an average of $2,356. Those from Australia and New Zealand, in closer proximity to the host country, spent on average $1,619, with 13.6 percent of them traveling business or first class by air, and those from other countries spent on average $1,359, with 9.3 percent of them booking business or first class flights. Note that they all spent more on fares than the usual average cost from their home country to Japan.

As a marketing consideration, it gave an opportunity to target offers related to a specific event of interest globally. Although these figures do not relate to age group of travelers, there would certainly be a mix of ages attending given the costs involved and timescales that those in full-time work would have to consider.

Barriers and Concerns to Address

Discussions so far have focused on identifying and defining the mature travel sector, looking at historical information to produce a customer profile that will support strategic marketing decisions. Their buying habits and preferred options for deciding what sort of trip they want, as well as where they might gain inspiration to try new brands, are a critical element of their final booking.

Before moving on to the discussion of further strategic options, it is necessary to look more closely at what the barriers are to the customer deciding to book a trip and the concerns they already have that might make them hesitate to go ahead and book with confidence.

Concerns

Concerns about the choice of destination persist. ATOL protection is higher on the list of concerns for UK travelers over the last three years, particularly with unknown changes following the Brexit agreement and withdrawal from membership of the EU (Silver Travel Advisor 2020). Travelers are worried about the increasing instability of travel providers, whether these are hotel chains, tour operators, or airlines—a major issue at the time of writing as the impact of COVID-19 travel bans become apparent. Some destinations are considered less safe at a personal level (crime, violence, political unrest), an issue regularly referred to by the more mature travelers. It is considered to be easier, and safer, to join a group or organized trip than book elements independently, so this may well have an impact on the growth of sites such as Expedia or Booking.com for this sector though not necessarily for younger age groups.

Customer Reviews

A closer look at the thousands of reviews posted on the Silver Travel Advisor website highlights the most common elements mature readers look out for from reviews of accommodation, travel, and package tours.

Reception and public areas, the first impression that a visitor gets on arrival, are a regular feature of what the mature customer is concerned about. Viewers of these reviews want to know whether the reception and check-in area is inviting—what are the first impressions? Is it a comfortable area to sit in and relax or is it draughty, small, and cramped or too dark?

A regular complaint about accommodation is that there is no lounge area separate from the music and entertainment areas, so conversation is impossible. Free Wi-Fi that can cope with the volume of guests on site is now expected by visitors globally, and one of the biggest issues is being charged for the service in the guest room with it only free in a public area. As the use of so many devices is now the norm across all age groups, this is increasingly a major concern for guests.

Lifts and stairs need to be accessible for those with large pieces of luggage or mobility aids, although it is important not to assume that "mature" means they automatically have disability or mobility issues as clearly this applies to all age groups.

Bathroom facilities are relevant irrespective of age group, so the main issue that arises is whether they are clean and that everything works. In the author's experience, poor water pressure, toilets that do not flush properly, or an immovable shower head seems to be a common occurrence!

Reviews regularly feature issues about noise between rooms, whether natural sounds such as snoring or other guests having the television on too loud late at night. Noisy plumbing systems are also mentioned frequently.

Noise outside the accommodation such as traffic or building works, which the hotel may not be able to control, is often cited as an issue. Noise inside the building, such as guest or staff room doors banging shut because no soft closures are fitted, is something that guests expect to be within the control of the accommodation provider.

They all sound like lots of small things, but they are the features that regularly appear and therefore present a negative review. The point is whether any senior staff member has ever stayed in one of their standard rooms overnight in order to appreciate why this feedback is important.

As each country or tour operator has their own criteria for allocating a star rating, it becomes more difficult for the customer to know what to expect and it potentially leads to negative feedback. Location is critical for any traveler, and the first impression basically confirms (or not) that it is where the provider said it was, whether in relation to town centers, travel links, or popular attractions. Comments are regularly based on transport links, particularly public transport in the home country if not traveling overseas, and transfer times from the port, airport, or rail station to the final destination.

Safety outside a resort, accommodation, or venue is important whatever the age group, but the issue is regularly raised in reviews. Whether city or rural locations, as mature travelers increasingly like to explore new places using public transport as well as on foot, it is inevitable that feeling wary of surroundings will add to negative review scores. This is not necessarily in the control of tour operators or service providers, but certainly local authorities do have to take it seriously as part of their tourism strategy.

Example

The main city areas in Malta are generally clean and tidy. However, St Paul's Bay is often dirty with trash collections ineffective. This has been more noticeable over the last three years. It makes it feel less safe though this is not necessarily the case, but it has been a real issue in many reviews even with travelers who have been visitors to the islands for many years.

It is important that people feel their views are taken on board by the service providers, yet experience suggests there is often a standard response from them saying "thank you for your positive feedback" even though it was anything but positive. Clearly the volume of responses from customers can be considerable, but it is a significant element of customer satisfaction.

Barriers

In the Solo Traveler World survey, "Reach the Solo Traveler", they found that 60 percent of adults who went on holiday alone in the last five years said they do not feel catered for. In both this survey (Solo Traveler World 2019) and that of Silver Travel Advisor, 52 percent of solo travelers said they were interested in an escorted tour and feel it is therefore safer and easier to see places that they would not travel to on their own.

The biggest barrier or negative issue facing solo travelers is the single supplement. Over half are put off booking because of the level of single supplement, and 69 percent said that the most important feature of trips they did book was that there was no supplement charged. Feedback from many sources suggests that they prefer to book a double room for single occupancy if possible as accommodation designated as single room is generally the worst in the hotel but may cost almost as much as a room for two people. When the choice is offered for a solo traveler to consider sharing, more than 77 percent said they would never share a room even with a same-sex person.

Supplement free is clearly the significant factor in making the final choice of where to go. Several cruise companies, such as Fred Olsen, have designated 10 percent of their cabins on certain liners for single use and Travelzoo features several partners who offer supplement-free trips.

Recent surveys also show that the new super-sized liners are not as attractive to many long-term cruise fans as was originally thought. Another issue associated with ocean cruising is additional costs on board (cited by 17 percent in Silver Travel Report 2020), whether these are transparent during the booking stage or not.

For those with mobility restrictions, 33 percent say transfer to and from airports and 25 percent say the airport itself presents difficulties, plus 20 percent cited access to attractions or events. For coach travel, the mature traveler is looking for smaller groups, more comfortable coaches, and therefore more at the luxury end of the coach travel market.

One of the biggest challenges for the mature traveler is the cost, or even availability, of travel insurance. Many providers finish standard insurance cover once you reach the age of 70; some providers in the UK have extended this to 80 years without additional cost (Barclays Bank plc current account Travel Plan, for example), but the biggest concern is about a declared existing condition.

Examples stated by survey respondents include the fact that because they have reached the birthday limit, they are now considered a bigger risk than they were the day before and insurance premiums went from £100 to £350! Many quotes refer to the "don't care" attitude of the travel industry and insurance providers, particularly where a long-term condition has been successfully managed for many years by standard medication—blood pressure or angina, for instance (Silver Travel Advisor 2020).

Given the demographic profiles at the beginning of this book, this is a serious issue that needs to be addressed. After all, this mature group is considered to be the one with high-level disposable income to spend on vacations and a keenness to travel and explore new places. For example, the Industry Report 2020 notes the range of quotes requested for insurance cover for 65+ include dogsledding, storm chasing, hang gliding, potholing, and heli-skiing. Interesting when you consider this alongside the earlier reference to most of the 60+ age group not recognizing themselves in adverts aimed at them.

Strategies

There are particular criteria that define the mature travel market and, as we have seen, particular elements of their demographic profile that differentiate between the 50+, 60+, 70+ age groups as well as lifestyle and travel preferences.

It would seem that segmentation is important, making sure there are hotels and accommodation facilities that meet the individual and group requirements. As we have seen already, it is vital that the potential customer feels comfortable with the persona presented by the company and that the company knows what they are looking for.

Rocky Mountaineer, the luxury train experience in Canada, recently carried out research to identify traveler profiles and find out what guests wanted from the onboard experience.

Around a third of guests (31 percent) identified with the "relaxed vacationer" persona of this luxury service. The majority of guests, 79 percent, agreed they read the onboard Milepost newspaper and 83 percent took it home with them (whether they had read it or not). A more significant finding for the company is that 68 percent felt that a digital app with real-time map and information would add to the whole onboard experience (Rocky Mountaineer 2020).

This persona of the brand can be further extended to reflect the characteristics of the region and tap into the perceptions of the visitor, whether real or imagined. This might be offering a stay in an historic chateau, castle, or manor house for customers seeking the romantic ideal. To the west of the UK, Wales has traditionally built tourism around ancient myths and legends, heroic princes and ruined castles, and the mystical atmosphere associated with mountains, lakes, and a rugged coastline. Each region around the world has its own persona or characteristics associated with it. To extend the reach and scope of future travel destinations for the mature sector, more specific marketing activities that link these elements of characteristics and persona with a new focus will, perhaps, be needed.

The reference to the persona of the brand, how the firm chooses to portray itself as someone the customer can relate to, is found in other examples. Amrita Gurney of CrowdRiff, for instance, discusses adding visual content to online marketing campaigns, particularly the importance of visual content that reflects the persona of the company, what they want to portray, and the different routes to reach the target customer. Several examples are quoted, including a clear rise of 28 percent in follow-through by visitors to a site when it changed the proportion of images from only using their own to a mix with user-generated images (UGIs).

UGIs have become more powerful as viewers are looking for examples of the "real" destination rather than what they see as more formal marketing images. While your own generated images are owned and controlled by you, high resolution and to your own specifications that can incorporate professionally made video material, there is often an impression that photographs produced by users of the facilities give a more realistic picture of what to expect.

Some interesting examples from CrowdRiff include a competition on social media for visitors to upload images of places not usually on the tourist trail of a city, a selection were chosen to go into a small booklet which then became so popular they had to repeat the competition and went on to publish many more copies. The result was that all places featured in the booklet saw an increase in visitors. Another example of a Visit Canada campaign, aimed at attracting U.S. tourists, used UGIs to produce a short video that resulted in an unprecedented increase in views of the site. Their latest article online discusses how to measure the impact of the visuals you choose to use in marketing campaigns (Gurney 2020).

We have seen how the use of UGI has grown in importance for those still at the planning stage. Although just outside our target age group, 72 percent of U.S. millennials refer to UGI to help them plan the content of their trip, so as they form the basis for future mature travel, it is an element that is likely to continue to grow.

Wish Trip Enterprise—a tourism experience management company based in Israel—has some valid points about brand and image management. They start from the premise that "Travelers are looking for unique experiences not necessarily pre-packaged deals," although as we have seen this may not necessarily be true for every part of the target mature sector.

As with CrowdRiff, they say that it is important for the brand to be associated with UGIs rather than standard marketing material. They stress that "emotional connection between destinations, visitors and others seeing the content" is then stronger. They have found that consistent branding can increase revenue by up to 23 percent, particularly if it includes as much in-destination content as possible (Hein 2020).

Wish Trip is also keen to encourage providing visitors with "digital trails" to follow on phone or the web, often including GPS navigation. They note that pdf downloads of map and trails are not necessarily useful for younger people who "don't know how to read a map!" Interesting to see how this would be received by the mature traveler who is more likely to be map-savvy. They have a tourism experience management platform which they say will help tour operators and providers track activities and demographic profiles of customers.

Some successful strategies already in place include tying trips in with significant dates during the year. World Cup (football or rugby) and other international sports events such as the Olympics have always seen a surge in demand for supporters to travel further afield. Japan was particularly positive about their role as host in 2019, for instance. In 2021, we recognize it is 120 years since the Commonwealth of Australia was formed and 245 years since the Declaration of Independence was signed in Philadelphia, United States.

Each year there are celebrations worldwide that can inspire the traveler to consider destinations they might not otherwise travel to (Titan Travel 2019–2020). The following list is just a small sample of celebrations or events that can be an added incentive for a prospective traveler to search online and go on to make a booking:

The Mardi Gras in New Orleans, United States, in February
The colorful Hindu festival of Holi in India in March
Stunning displays of tulips in the Netherlands in April
The Inca Festival of the Sun in Peru, South America, in June
The exciting Calgary Stampede in Canada in July
Being part of the grape harvest in Douro Valley, Portugal, in September
Whale watching off the coast of South Africa in October

Summary

As we have seen, booking any form of travel or package is a complex process for the customer who has so many variables to consider before making a final choice. Unlike anyone using an online platform to buy a specific product, it is not so straightforward to compare, say, dimensions or properties of a product such as a dishwasher in the same way as you would an overseas trip for a solo or mature couple traveler. If the typical time scale for starting to research and book a vacation is three to six months, as noted in the ATTEST Travel Report (Attest 2019), this is generally not an impulse buy.

The ATTEST Travel Report 2019 covers a wider demographic, but it also identifies significant points that need to inform any future strategy. The main findings for the 55+ age group are that they are less concerned about the stated star rating for accommodation or a package tour, preferring to make their choice based on reviews and images, but social media had the least impact on their final decision to make a booking. The point was also made that bed and breakfast or all-inclusive packages are the preferred option, a smaller proportion preferring self-catering facilities, but across all age groups in the survey the vast majority were not interested in booking half board or full board packages without access to drinks and snacks included in the price. This is a growing shift in booking preferences and will have an impact on development of future offerings to the client sector.

Some of the main points that have emerged from our analysis include the "obvious" ones to those already in marketing professions. However, the analysis also highlights more recent changes in customer buying habits of the mature traveler that should be part of future strategic decisions. The main points include:

- Be specific about who the target actually is. This may be by age group, but this must be broader than a category of 50+, 60+, or 70+. There are more specific criteria that better reflect the potential customer.
- What is the best route to reach them? We have already seen that e-mail is still a favorite method and various social media platforms a growing avenue to find out about new brands. This is particularly important at the planning stage and also to reinforce their views about the various options they are considering.
- Hard copy continues to be an effective way to reach customers and has a longer shelf life. It is potentially more expensive to produce but serves as a reminder to the potential customer of what is available when they are still at the research and planning stage.
- As travel agents continue to be the preferred choice for booking a package or more complicated set of requirements, clearly hard copy continues to be a vital element for them to showcase options.

It is interesting that different surveys have found the mature traveler is really not impressed by celebrity endorsement! While younger groups are avid followers of celebrity endorsements on social media, it is vital that it is not assumed to be worth the spend for the mature target group. As before, personal safety and security is a critical issue for all travel agents and tour operators to consider.

Overtourism

Overtourism is increasingly an issue the travel sector must take on board in future marketing strategies. Already the most popular destinations, including Venice, Barcelona, and Maya Bay in Thailand, are either closing to large-scale cruise or package tours or restricting visitor numbers so the tourist sector must take care of how they offer such options.

City breaks are consistently seen as a favorite option for the mature traveler, but these major city attractions, and many other European destinations, are now suffering significant problems with the supporting infrastructure. The impact of high volumes of tourists on local residents, particularly numbers of short-term visitors when a cruise ship docks for just a day, cannot be ignored.

The list of the most visited monuments in the world in 2019 (K. Buchholz, statista.com) included The Forbidden City in Beijing, China, in first place followed by Versailles Palace in France and the Taj Mahal in India, although it was noted that waiting times for these attractions run into many hours. The National Mall in Washington DC is a regular feature of "most visited" lists as are the Eiffel Tower in Paris and Sagrada Familia in Barcelona, Spain. Even rural areas are suffering from overtourism, seeing a continuous stream of walkers on long-distance designated paths or the exposed ridges along the top of hills and mountains, all showing clear signs of erosion and damage requiring constant maintenance and repair.

It does require a concerted effort by tour operators and service providers to ensure such places can continue to be enjoyed by tourists from around the world without destroying them in the process. For the 60+ mature traveler, the most popular attractions may not necessarily represent a problem as they are seeking new and different places to visit. As a target sector, finding new locations is, therefore, a significant opportunity.

Ecotourism

There is a growing movement among tourists and tour operators to show how tourism is benefiting local communities visited. This is a positive element for tour operators who include content that draws on skills of the local people, helps their local charities, and uses local guides wherever possible (Titan Travel 2019–2020). The ABTA report also found 50 percent of respondents thought the green credentials of the provider important or essential when choosing their trip, and 62 percent specifically wanted travel companies to ensure the visit helps local people and their economy (ABTA 2019).

This eco-friendly factor is not just a Western issue but something visitors to Asia, Africa, South America, and the Far East are asking about. Train travel is a good example of choice made on the basis of environmental impact—"train bragging" the journey not the destination (Condé Nast)—but is also a more leisurely way to explore a new destination. Slower travel means more time to connect and spend money with the local community and businesses. The train is a greener option than air travel, of course, with electric trains showing even lower CO_2 emissions.

Sustainable travel is high on the agenda for both travelers and providers within the tourism sectors. Globally, those in the mature age groups are taking more vacations, trips are perhaps more varied than previously, and whichever country of origin, people are spending more money. The crucial trend into the future is sustainability—a difficult issue when considering air travel, although airlines are searching for lower emissions through new technologies.

The various elements of "sustainability" must include reference to the environmental, social, and economic impact, with 87 percent of tourists preferring brands that demonstrate their commitment to a sustainable approach (J.W. Thomson [Condé Nast 2019]). For instance, G Adventures shows "ripple scores" that represent the proportion of the tour's spend that stays in the destination. ABTA's 2019 campaign "Make Holidays Greener" involves commitment to waste management through Reduce–Reuse–Recycle.

The industry is trying its best to counteract some of the negative elements of worldwide travel, although this may seem to be at a more superficial level, such as reducing use of single-use plastics, using compostable packaging where possible, and encouraging individuals to reduce their own throw-away habits. However, this must be seen against the backdrop of overtourism we have already seen in earlier sections.

In the first two decades of the 21st century, the focus on environmental protection is a growing concern for the public and for the tourist industry as a whole. Air travel remains a concern, but destinations are increasingly stressing the measures they take to be eco-friendly as this appears regularly as an issue when making the final holiday choice.

While luxury-end providers can ensure their accommodation uses energy-efficient equipment and they can show they care about the use of natural resources (such as Maxx Royal Resorts in Turkey that feature this in their advertising campaigns [Condé Nast 2019]), this is not always the case at economy-level resorts and accommodation. It must be a significant element of any future strategy at a global level.

Responsible tourism is becoming the mantra worldwide and must be acknowledged by all sectors. Demand is increasing, this demographic of 50+ age group is clearly expanding as is their desire, and ability, to visit the attractions on their "bucket list." Less likely to be in full-time work (although around half a million over 60 years are in full- or part-time employment), longer trips are a possibility including "gap years" for older travelers. Clearly there is potential to expand tourism and identify new and exciting destinations in the future for many mature travelers (USTOA). They represent 60 percent of travel spend and are likely to book earlier, at least six months before the planned trip—so there are lots of opportunities for targeted marketing material.

What of the Future?

There is a feeling that while some less-populated destinations are opening up, many of the popular long-term "must see" places are becoming restricted and actually reducing globally. Overtourism does not help, and while travelers are seeking more undiscovered, eco-friendly destinations, experience suggests such places do not remain "undiscovered" for very long. As we have seen, cities such as Rome, Venice, Amsterdam, Lisbon, Dubrovnik are trying to find ways to manage the negative impact on their infrastructure. While we know long-haul flights may be problematic, many of the destinations involved do rely heavily on income from tourism.

So, while new and exciting destinations are opening up, the demand for access to the well-known tourist attractions worldwide continues with no sign of reducing. Nevertheless, the industry has to find a way to balance this demand with the need to take environmental damage and erosion seriously.

This particular sector appears to be forever curious, bucket lists are getting longer, and they are looking for cultural experiences, adventure, and a wide range of activities as vacation content. Multigeneration breaks are likely to increase, probably including three to four generations to celebrate milestone events or anniversaries. Cruising is continuing to grow in popularity as the choice between no-fly ocean cruises or fly to pick up point for the start of the cruise opens up and appeals to a wider group of new passengers.

There will need to be more accessible holiday provision and as the aging population will inevitably grow, there will also need to be more solo holidays for single travelers.

As the "wish list" or "bucket list" would appear to be changing in content, emphasis, and importance, it represents an opportunity for all those in travel/tourism industries to demonstrate their commitment to assisting clients in finding their dream trip while protecting an increasingly fragile planet.

The global impact of the COVID-19 Pandemic

At the beginning of 2020, a major coronavirus flu epidemic emerged and made travel to or from China and the Far East almost impossible. As the COVID-19 virus spread globally, at an unprecedented rapid pace (at the time of writing), there has been a significant, and in many cases devastating, impact on all travel plans, whether for leisure or business, and for tourist destinations all around the world.

Everyone involved in tourism and travel industries have been affected, particularly the airline, cruise, and hospitality sectors that have been particularly hard-hit. An in-depth analysis of the impact of COVID-19 is outside the remit for this book, but a further volume in 2021 will consider "Tourism and COVID19" in more detail.

There are many questions about the potential outcome for the industry that cannot be answered at this time.

Demographic Changes

There is evidence already that the death rate from the virus is higher among the older generations globally. It is not restricted to this age group of course, but it will be interesting to see how the demographic profiles of countries featured in this book will change. In the UK, there is a census of the population every 10 years. This is due to take place in 2021 so will provide data for the ONS that can be compared with previous figures discussed here (ONS 2018–2019).

Economic Impact

Changes to investments and potentially pension funds can have a major impact for the mature sector, reducing available funds for travel. This can lead to reducing the number of trips taken each year and the annual spend. In addition, many businesses are trying to find ways to deal with the downturn and unemployment is rising, so again, this can have an impact on the leisure sectors.

Ecotourism

Will the restrictions on travel currently in place change the views of mature travelers as we are already seeing a positive impact on nature and wildlife as travel-related pollution falls? It can have a major impact on how and when we travel as well as on the choice of destinations.

Impact on Travel and Tourism

It remains to be seen what the sector will look like at the end of the crisis. New marketing strategies will be needed to accommodate such fundamental changes to attitudes, buying habits, and choices customers will need to make if their circumstances alter significantly.

While this book was written before the pandemic took hold globally, it is now vitally important that providers step back and start to reconsider their marketing strategies to be fully prepared for when it all ends. But at some stage people will be able to travel again.

Bibliography and Reference Sources

ABTA. 2019. *ABTA*. Retrieved from Association of British Travel Agents: www.abta.com

ADARA. 2019. *Travel Marketing Strategies.* https://travelmassive.com/adara

Ahmad, J. 2019. *Understanding people and brands: paper at MMA conference.* Retrieved from Accord Marketing: htpp://accordmarketing.com

ASTA. 2020. *American Society of Travel Agents (ASTA).* Retrieved from tourismnotes.com: www.tourismnotes.com

ATTEST. 2019. *Generational Trends Report 2019.* www.askattest.com

Attest. 2019. *Travel Report 2019.* www.askattest.com

Aurora Zone. 2019. Retrieved from The Aurora Zone/Artisan Travel Company: www.theaurorazone.com

Booking.com. 2020. Retrieved from Booking.com: www.booking.com

Condé Nast. 2019. The Gold List 2020. *Conde Nast traveller.*

Condor Ferries. 2020. *Home Page for Travel Information.* Retrieved from Condor Ferries: www.condorferries.co.uk

Crisp, L. 2019. *Member Profiles.* Retrieved from Gransnet: www.gransnet.com

DMA. 2019. *Acquisition and the Consumer Mindset.* www.dma.org.uk

DMA. 2019. *Winning Trust & Building Loyalty.* www.dma.org.uk

DMA. 2020. *Consumer Email Tracker 2020 Report.* Retrieved from DMA: www.dma.org.uk

ETOA . 2019. Retrieved from European Tourism Association: www.etoa.org

expedia.com. 2020. *Expedia.com.* Retrieved from www.expedia.com

EyeforTravel. 2020. *Tracking Users Across All Devices.* Retrieved from eyefortravel.com: www.eyefortravel.com

Gurney, A. 2020. *Visual Marketing Masterclass.* Retrieved from Crowdriff.com: www.crowdriff.com

Hein, S. 2020. *Tourism Experience Management*. Retrieved from Wish-Trip Enterprise: http:www.wishtrip.com

Jeynes, J. 2017. *Walking Wales: The Art Lover's Guide to Wye Valley Way*. www.pencoedpublishing.co.uk

Johnson, P. 2020. *Travel Blog*. Retrieved from Luxury Travel Blog: www.aluxurytravelblog.com

Keeley, A. 2019. Target Markets. *Travel Weekly Mature Travel*, 7. www.travelweekly.co.uk

Mail Metro Media Travel Team. 2019. *Mail Metro Media Travel Survey 2019*. Mail Metro Media. www.mailmetromedia.co.uk

MMA, Mature Marketing Association. *The MMA Marketing Summit*. London: MMA. www.themma.marketing

Oddfellows. 2019. *Active Travel Club Update*. London: Oddfellows. www.oddfellows.co.uk

ONS. 2018–2019. Retrieved from Office for National Statistics: www.ons.gov.uk

Ramblers Holidays. 2020. *Cruise and Walk Holidays*. Retrieved from Ramblers Holidays: www.ramblersholidays.co.uk

Rocky Mountaineer. 2020. Retrieved from Rocky Mountaineer: www.rockymountaineer.com

Silver Travel Advisor. 2020. *Silver Travel Advisor*. Retrieved from www.silvertraveladvisor.com

Silver Travel Advisor. 2020. *Silver Travel Report 2020*.

Solo Traveler World. 2019. Reach the Solo Travel Market. *Solo Traveler World*. www.solotravelerworld.com

Statista. 2020. *Studies and Reports*. Retrieved from Statista: www.statista.com

Statistics Poland/ Statista. 2019. *Visitors to Poland*. Retrieved from stat.gov.pl: www.stat.gov.pl

Targett, L. 2019. *Social Influencers – Paper for MMA Conference*. Retrieved from TRIBE: www.tribegroup.co

The Trainline.com. 2019. *European Travel*. Retrieved from Trainline.com: www.trainline.com

Titan Travel. 2019–2020. *Travel Trends 2020*. Titan Travel. www.titantravel.co.uk

Travel Weekly. 2019. *Mature Travel Report*. www.travelweekly.co.uk

Travelzoo. 2019. Retrieved from Travelzoo.com: www.travelzoo.com

Trip Advisor. 2019. *Most Booked Destinations for US Tourists 2019.* Retrieved from Trip Advisor: www.tripadvisor.com

Unsplash. 2020. *Photo Images.* Retrieved from Unsplash.com: www .unsplash.com

US Travel Association. 2019. Retrieved from US Travel Association: www.ustravel.org

USTOA. 2018. *USTOA Membership Contrributes $19 billion to Travel Industry.* Retrieved from US Tour Operators Association (USTOA): www.ustoa.com

Worldmeters. 2020. *Worldmeters/Demographic.* Retrieved from Worldmeters: www.worldmeters.info

About the Author

Dr Jacqueline Jeynes PhD, MBA, BEd(Hons), BA(Hons)

Dr Jeynes is the author of a range of nonfiction titles based on her experience in several business and creative sectors.

She is a travel writer with a focus on mature travel sectors covering tour packages, travel and accommodation, food and wine, theater, and entertainment. She regularly writes reviews for Silver Travel Advisor plus full-scale reports (3,000 words) on particular destinations, hotel chains, and as part of press trips for tour operators.

She has published a travel book *Walking Wales: The Art Lover's Guide to Wye Valley Way* as part of a series and is currently working on a two-part series of books *A Meander through Wales* using bus, train, and on foot, which is directly related to the current move to reduce an individual's carbon footprint.

Her books include *Practical Health and Safety Management for Small Firms* as well as academic titles such as *10 Principles of Risk Management*, based on her PhD that covers these sectors. She was awarded Specialist Business Adviser of the Year from the Institute of Business Advisers and Writer of the Year (Non-fiction) from Writing Magazine.

Dr Jeynes has worked with several universities, as a tutor on Durham University distance learning MBA and as a tutor for Aston University Business degree students on their one-year industry placement. This program includes students preparing an individual study of a business problem, using academic theory to analyze it, then saying how useful the theory actually is in the real world, thus covering a wide range of industry sectors.

Since 1987 she has been running her own management training consultancy, writer, and a tutor for degree level distance learning modules for Aberystwyth University and the Open College of the Arts.

She is an Authority member and book reviewer for the Non-Fiction Author's Association (NFAA) and started her own small publishing company in 2015 acting as editor and publisher. She lives in Wales with her husband Leslie.

Contact: jackiepencoed@gmail.com

Website: www.jacquelinejeynes.com; www.pencoedpublishing.co.uk

www.twitter.com/jackiepencoed; www.facebook.com/jacquelinejeynes

Index

OTHER TITLES IN THE TOURISM AND HOSPITALITY MANAGEMENT COLLECTION

Betsy Bender Stringam, New Mexico State University, *Editor*

- *Improving Convention Center Management Using Business Analytics and Key Performance Indicators: Advanced Practices* by Myles T. McGrane
- *Improving Convention Center Management Using Business Analytics and Key Performance Indicators: Focusing on Fundamentals* by Myles T. McGrane
- *A Profile of the Hospitality Industry, Second Edition* by Betsy Bender Stringam
- *Cultural and Heritage Tourism and Management* by Tammie J. Kaufman
- *Marketing Essentials for Independent Lodging* by Pamela Lanier
- *Marine Tourism, Climate Change, and Resilience in the Caribbean, Volume II, Recreation, Yachts, and Cruise Ships* by Kreg Ettenger
- *Marine Tourism, Climate Change, and Resiliency in the Caribbean, Volume I, Ocean Health, Fisheries, and Marine Protected Areas* by Kreg Ettenger
- *Catering and Convention Service Survival Guide in Hotels and Casinos* by Lisa Lynn Backus
- *Coastal Tourism, Sustainability, and Climate Change in the Caribbean, Volume II, Supporting Activities* by Martha Honey
- *Coastal Tourism, Sustainability, and Climate Change in the Caribbean, Volume I, Beaches and Hotels* by Martha Honey
- *The Good Company: Sustainability in Hospitality, Tourism and Wine* by Robert Girling

Concise and Applied Business Books

The Collection listed above is one of 30 business subject collections that Business Expert Press has grown to make BEP a premiere publisher of print and digital books. Our concise and applied books are for...

- Professionals and Practitioners
- Faculty who adopt our books for courses
- Librarians who know that BEP's Digital Libraries are a unique way to offer students ebooks to download, not restricted with any digital rights management
- Executive Training Course Leaders
- Business Seminar Organizers

Business Expert Press books are for anyone who needs to dig deeper on business ideas, goals, and solutions to everyday problems. Whether one print book, one ebook, or buying a digital library of 110 ebooks, we remain the affordable and smart way to be business smart. For more information, please visit **www.businessexpertpress.com**, or contact **sales@businessexpertpress.com**.

www.ingramcontent.com/pod-product-compliance
Lightning Source LLC
Chambersburg PA
CBHW061325220326
41599CB00026B/5040